WEARING THE RUBY SLIPPERS:
NINE STEPS TO HAPPINESS

Dr Kristina Downing-Orr was born in Boston, but has lived in the UK since 1986. She has studied at Oxford, London and Birmingham Universities and works as a clinical psychologist. She is also a novelist, playwright, humourist and broadcaster.

Also by Kristina Downing-Orr

101 Reasons Why Your Man's from Heaven and from Hell
(Robinson 2003)
The Tap Dancer's Shadow
(Iumix 2003)
Get The Life You Want
(Thorsons 2000)
What to Do if You're Burnt Out and Blue
(Thorsons 2000)
Rethinking Depression: Why Current Treatments Fail
(Planum 1998)
Alienation and Social Support
(Avebury 1996)
Shrink Resistant – A Play
(Stratford Playscrips 2003)

WEARING THE RUBY SLIPPERS

NINE STEPS TO HAPPINESS

Dr Kristina Downing-Orr

arrow books

Published by Arrow Books in 2003

3 5 7 9 10 8 6 4

Copyright © Dr Kristina Downing-Orr

Arrow Books Limited
The Random House Group Limited
20 Vauxhall Bridge Road, London SW1V 2SA

Random House Australia (Pty) Limited
20 Alfred Street, Milsons Point, Sydney,
New South Wales 2061, Australia

Random House New Zealand Limited
18 Poland Road, Glenfield
Auckland 10, New Zealand

Random House (Pty) Limited
Endulini, 5a Jubilee Road, Parktown 2193, South Africa

The Random House Group Limited Reg. No. 954009

www.randomhouse.co.uk

A CIP catalogue record for this book
is available from the British Library

Penguin Random House is committed to a sustainable future for
our business, our readers and our planet. This book is made from
Forest Stewardship Council® certified paper.

Printed and bound in Great Britain by Clays Ltd, Elcograf S.p.A.

ISBN 9780099456988

Designed by Roger Walker

Typeset by SX Composing DTP, Rayleigh, Essex

The author and publisher have made all reasonable efforts to contact
copyright holders for permission and apologise for any omissions or errors
in the form of credits given. Corrections may be made to future printings.

Acknowledgements

There are many people who've inspired and assisted me throughout the entirety of this book. The late Michael Argyle, Professor Michael Eysenck and the work of Robert Holden were particularly influencial to my work. An extra thank-you to Michael Eysenck for his kind permission. Hannah Black and Mark Booth, my editors, remained great sources of enthusiasm throughout. Finally, special mention must go to my many clients throughout the years whose experiences and human dilemmas have shaped the foundation for my work.

Finding True Happiness the CBT Way

The gall of Madame de Gaulle . . .

Legend famously has it that the widow of General Charles de Gaulle was once interviewed by a glittering gathering of dignitaries, politicians and journalists on what she wanted most in life. 'Happiness,' she asserted with great and gleeful resolve, much to the shock, horror and sheer consternation of the assembled luminaries.

You're probably puzzled, right? After all, why should Madame de Gaulle's straightforward and perfectly reasonable request for personal joy cause jaws to drop and feet to shuffle awkwardly on that day? Surely there is nothing so unusual or particularly odd in a desire for happiness? Well, yes and, er, um, no. You see, there was a slight breakdown in communication that day. The eminent general's widow spoke English with a strong French accent – dropping the 'h' and stressing the second syllable. And, without drawing a diagram, instead of conveying her wish for a life imbued with joy, Madame de Gaulle erroneously gave the impression she desired something else! Well, I suppose she was French.

Saucy linguistic mishaps aside, most people would probably

agree that being happy is pretty high up on their list of priorities. How about you? Is happiness important to you? If so, can you honestly say you're really happy with your life? I mean, truly fulfilled? Take a few moments now, if you would, for a good, long, candid look at your personal circumstances. Is your life turning out to be as fulfilling, exciting, rewarding and successful as you hoped? Or does even the mere suggestion of assessing your current situation fill you with despondency?

If you're less than satisfied with your lot in life, you are far from alone. Despite the fact that many men and women pinpoint 'being happy' as a major priority – in fact, the right to pursue happiness is guaranteed as an 'unalienable right' in the American Declaration of Independence – unfortunately misery still seems to be widespread. Yet life lived well is full of tremendous beauty, wonder, humanity and joy. The trouble is most of us are so immersed in and blinkered by our daily grind – commuting, working, paying bills, worrying about finances, dealing with the stresses and strains of modern living – not to mention bombarded with bleak social forecasts, we're in real danger of failing to enjoy and appreciate our very limited time on this extraordinary planet.

What's more, many people confess to me that even if they could somehow magically sweep away all their stresses and strains, the trouble is they've actually *forgotten* how to be happy and wouldn't have the first clue how to take a step in that direction. For almost two decades now, I've worked as a cognitive behavioural therapist with countless and diverse groups of men and women, many of whom have convinced themselves they're incapable of ever being happy. That they are beyond help. That happiness happens to other people, not to them. They all tell me they've tried, they really have. They've played the game. Followed the rules. Worked hard. Made sacrifices. Juggled the demands of career, families and degree courses. They've done all 'the right things', but somehow happiness always seems to elude them. Even those high-flying clients of mine who've reached a point in their lives when they should be enjoying the fruits of their labours and savouring their achievements, instead spend time counting the costs of that success – to their relationships, their health and, paradoxically, their self-esteem. Who can blame them for feeling frustrated and confused?

For some reason, the expensive cars, palatial homes, the exotic vacations and designer clothes, far from making them happy, often leave them feeling empty and disillusioned, hankering for something more personally meaningful and challenging. Since success is supposed to be the foundation of happiness, they demand, then why do they constantly feel so miserable?

Here's what some of them have said to me:

> In the past few years, I married a terrific man, gave birth to a beautiful little girl and I love my job. I'm the envy of my friends and I know I should be happy, but my life feels flat. I wasn't really expecting 'happy ever after' once I found my knight in shining armour. But I'm so busy every day, I'm on this constant treadmill and just feel like a drudge. What's worse is I feel guilty. I've got everything. What right do I have to complain?

> I've had a really difficult year. My marriage ended and I lost my job and I feel more and more isolated. I try to keep a positive attitude, look on the bright side, keep smiling, but usually I just end up feeling worse.

> I've worked hard all my life. Went to the right schools, chose the right career path, joined the right clubs. I thought all these things would make me happy, but they don't. I don't want to sound all New-Agey, but recently I've been feeling like my life should amount to more than just the grand total of my achievements.

I've spent so much time dedicated to my career that my teenage children are like strangers to me. They'll all be leaving home soon and I know so little about them. Or them me. To them, I'm just a wallet, the one who hands out the money. I hate being a stranger in my own family.

About a year ago, I decided to lose weight. I'd put on the pounds since having my children and hated being fat. I exercised and dieted my way down to a size ten from a twenty-two. I love the way I look, not to mention all the attention I get, but then I start to think. I know I should be happy, but I'm the same person inside as I always was. It makes me sad that people only respond to my looks. That I only have any worth because I'm thin.

I always used to think I'd be happy when I achieved my goals. I'd be happy when I finished my degree. I'd be happy when I found my dream job. When I bought my first car, house, etc. And I am, but the feelings never seem to last too long. Am I just incapable of finding permanent happiness?

Happiness is all down to luck, isn't it? Some people are born with all the cards stacked in their favour, but with others it's a misdeal every time.

These are real people, with very real, very painful problems and dilemmas. And I bet that some of their thoughts and fears resonate with you. If so, then you know full well that these men and women can't be dismissed as mere misery merchants.

The people I work with are ordinarily pleasant, stable and grounded. They tend to be hard-working and committed to their families and careers. But they feel genuinely disappointed, not to mention cheated, because despite their dedication, hard work and effort, happiness and personal fulfilment continue to elude them.

One client summed up what he felt and I think his words would resonate with just about everyone else I've come across in this situation:

> I know it sounds silly, but I always expected life was going to be a bit like the Coca-Cola adverts. Good friends, fun times, great parties, great job. But life's not like that. I saw a slogan on a T-shirt the other day: Birth, school, work, death. Surely, there's more to life than that. Isn't there?

THE TRUTH MAY BE OUT THERE, BUT WHAT ABOUT HAPPINESS?

Perhaps you, too, have reached a similar conclusion. Maybe you feel your situation is pretty bleak, hopeless even. But take heart, it's not. I promise. In the course of my work as a psychologist specialising in cognitive behavioural therapy (CBT), I've helped many men and women achieve happier, more fulfilling existences. Lives full of possibility and contentment they never dreamed imaginable.

So, what would you think if I said I could do the same for you? If you're like many people I encounter professionally, you're probably sitting there right now, rolling your eyes and shaking your head dismissively.

After all, while there are a number of very good, very insightful, very well-researched and -written self-help books out there on the shelves, sadly there are also quite a few duds around. You probably know some of the titles I mean.

That's why I *want* you to be highly sceptical about my claims and make me work to earn your trust and your attention. When it comes to your own well-being, it never hurts to be discerning. Why exactly is this book a cut above the rest?

Well, I'm a qualified clinical psychologist who every day helps people like you resolve their personal difficulties and improve their sense of well-being. I'm also an academic, with two doctorates (from Oxford and Birmingham Universities), who regularly conducts research and publishes on a wide range of mental health matters for my professional peers – not an easy crowd to please – and the general public.

Also, when I'm not wearing my clinical or research hat, I'm usually working as a corporate consultant, specialising in leadership, negotiation, conflict resolution, creativity and problem-solving, motivation, and presentation. I also broadcast on television and radio as a psychology and social affairs commentator?

So, my academic background means I can sniff out inane psychobabble a mile off and am up-to-date on all the current research literature in psychology; daily clinical work with men and women of all ages and backgrounds guarantees there's no danger of the out-of-touch, ivory tower about me; and frequent grilling on television and radio by inquisitive broadcasters means my views must be cohesive, well-prepared and articulate or else I face public humiliation. Drawing on this accumulated expertise, I wrote *Wearing The Ruby Slippers*.

WEARING THE RUBY WHAT?!?

Yes, I admit, it's a curious, even whimsical title, but there's a method to my madness. As just about everyone over the age of five will immediately comprehend, the title of this book was inspired by the much-loved movie classic *The Wizard of Oz*, for a number of reasons.

In my view, since the aim of this book is to help you develop a greater sense of happiness and well-being, the movie's magical plot, with all its twists and turns and tribulations, serves as a poetic metaphor for everyday human experience and striving for personal fulfilment. Like so many people I work with and know, the film's characters have clear, firm ideas about their personal goals and dreams at the start of their journey. However, even though they're all highly motivated and committed to pursuing their ambitions, they are beset with problems and setbacks at every point.

Let's look at the lovable foursome and how their experiences relate to 'real life'. We'll start with Dorothy. Is this girl a minefield of teenage angst or what? Right from the opening scenes of the film, it's obvious she is suffering from an acute case of the emotional growing pains universal to adolescents everywhere. Let's look at the evidence. She feels completely misunderstood and unloved by her family. She believes she's a nuisance who only causes trouble and gets in everyone's way. She fantasises about faraway places 'somewhere over the rainbow' where 'dreams really do come true'. And she runs away from home in a bid to find this magical place.

Dorothy's journey through Oz is a voyage of personal discovery. The hardships and dangers she faces not only help her grow up, but also give her valuable insights into her family relationships. Compared to the wicked witches hovering above the Emerald City, that humble little farm in Kansas doesn't seem like such a bad bet after all and her attachments to her family are strengthened by this new understanding. So much so, she vows never to leave her 'own backyard' to go in search of happiness again, because everything she ever needed was already there. Dorothy just had to learn that for herself.

Her colourful cohorts all also gain valuable personal insight from their adventures. Like Dorothy, it was their negative perceptions of themselves that held them back and made them truly unhappy. And all despite overwhelming evidence to the contrary! They were so busy doing themselves down, they didn't stop and check out whether or not their damaging, destructive self-beliefs were even true.

The Scarecrow thinks he's nothing more than a dim-witted bag of straw. The Tinman is convinced he is just a hunk of junk, incapable of feeling. The Cowardly Lion really, truly believes he is a quivering nervous wreck, terrified of his own shadow. And yet throughout the entirety of the film each character abundantly demonstrates the very traits he thinks he so egregiously lacks – even in the most threatening and challenging of circumstances. The Scarecrow's intelligence is revealed when the chips are down and Dorothy is locked up in the evil witch's castle. He is instrumental in hatching the escape plot. The Tinman bangs on an empty, hollow metallic chest, but shows nothing but an outpouring of love, support and loyalty to his friends even when his own life is endangered. And true valour? Far from being the lily-livered, craven laughing stock he fears, the Cowardly Lion proves time and time again that he can confront his worst fears and stand strong in the face of danger. The characters' self-assessment reflects the power of our own negative beliefs. Dorothy and her friends all need to learn that they aren't quite as incompetent, insignificant, unlovable or unworthy as they believe they are. Just the opposite, in fact.

Negative self-esteem is pretty persistent stuff. Back in Oz, even though their innumerable personal strengths were obvious to others, these characters still wouldn't take them on board themselves. They needed the endorsement of the Wizard to boost their self-esteem and give them the validation they desperately craved. The Scarecrow got his sheepskin, the Tinman a ticking clock as a symbol of his beating heart, the Cowardly Lion his medals. While the Wizard was wily and loathsome in many respects, he did revealingly point out that the trinkets he gave them were nothing but tokens, reflecting and celebrating qualities they already possessed within themselves.

Like Dorothy and her friends, my clients have often been

seeking to find personal happiness in all the wrong places and in all the wrong ways. Frequently, most definitely, they discount and ignore their own abilities and inner resources when trying to achieve their ambitions and goals. Sadly, in real life, wizards don't often pass their way, pointing out their hidden strengths. Instead, I encourage people to investigate CBT.

Finding happiness the CBT way

Cognitive behavioural therapy, or CBT as it's more widely known, is about the best thing to hit the world since sliced bread. Well, okay, the shrink world anyway. Since its introduction in the late-sixties, it's no exaggeration to say that CBT has revolutionised the way psychologists help their clients understand and resolve their personal difficulties. Why is CBT so highly regarded? Simple. It's easier than rival therapies to learn and apply, equips us with effective problem-solving skills, shows us how to take control of our lives and overcome even our worst nightmares. As every clinician knows, CBT is nothing short of life-transforming.

The therapy was originally designed by Dr Aaron Beck to help people overcome clinical depression, but its practices, principles and skills are now much more widely used in the successful treatment of a whole host of other problems including phobias, eating disorders, anxieties, relationship difficulties, addictions, sleep disturbances. So vastly influential is CBT nowadays in the clinical realm that it has become the treatment of choice for mental health professionals around the world, has far eclipsed all other mainstream traditional therapies, and dominates the theoretical agendas of research studies into all areas of human behaviour. To give you some idea of CBT's pervasiveness, figures are now indicating that between about 60 and 80 percent of all clinical treatment is conducted from this therapeutic basis.

Until now, however, the empowering, life-enhancing tools and techniques of CBT have remained the sole preserve of the clinicians and, therefore, been unavailable to the millions of men and women everywhere who have had no personal experience or real need of the professional's couch.

Well, not any more. while CBT may traditionally have been designed for clinical patients, everyone can benefit from its skills and teachings. No matter what personal challenges they face. No matter what changes they'd like or need to make.

A BRIEF HISTORY OF MIND (WITH APOLOGIES TO STEPHEN HAWKING)

I've worked as a psychologist for a number of years now and have been schooled in all the major areas of psychological therapies: psychoanalysis, behaviourism, humanistic, social/community, Rogerian and cognitive. I have worked with countless people, both as patients and as corporate clients, and have found that most of them respond best to my cognitive behavioural approach when helping them identify, analyse and overcome their problems.

Before we delve any deeper into the exciting practices and principles of CBT, I think it might be useful to put this approach into some kind of perspective. A little psycho-history, if you like.

Freudian Psychoanalysis

Let's start at the very beginning . . . with psychoanalysis. Everyone and their grandmother's heard of Sigmund Freud, patron saint and guru of pretty much every therapist around the world. He pioneered the science of psychology in the latter part of the nineteenth century and early years of the twentieth, and without so much as a hint of modesty proclaimed himself the 'conquistador of the mind'.

Levels of consciousness

In a nutshell, Freud reasoned that all human behaviours are governed predominantly by our innate sexual or aggressive impulses. These tendencies we regard as so repulsive and ugly we don't like to admit we experience them or even own up to having them in the first place. So threatening are these bestial impulses, we tend instead to prefer locking them away, deep within our subconscious. A kind of intrapsychic out of sight, out of mind.

For the most part, we are fairly successful at controlling these unspeakable, unpalatable drives and get on with managing to live our lives. However, every once in a while these impulses breach our carefully guarded subconscious fortresses and cause us trouble such as phobias, obsessive-compulsive disorders and anxiety.

The chief aim of psychoanalysis, a type of psychotherapy originated by Freud, is to help us uncover the precise unconscious causes at the root of our particular psychological distress.

Freud wrote that all our behaviours, whether normal or abnormal, are governed by unconscious psychological motives. In other words, even our seemingly unintentional or inadvertent behaviours can be explained by what he deemed psychic determinism, leading one psychologist to observe 'the forgotten lunch engagement, the slip of the tongue, the barked shin could no longer be dismissed as an accident'. No doubt we've all had experiences of the 'Freudian Slip'.

How do we get these unconscious sexual and aggressive impulses in the first place? Freud claimed that early-childhood experiences are the most important factors in shaping our behaviour as adults. He argued that memories of these experiences were stored in the unconscious mind and continued to impact on our responses throughout our lives.

So, if our personalities are formed then, what do they consist of? In psychoanalytic terms, our personalities are composed of three distinct structures. According to Freud, these are called the id, the ego and the superego, and are buried deep within our unconscious.

The id is the part of us that houses all our basic innate motives, drives, appetites and impulses. You might say the id is the spoiled, amoral, impulsive brat whose mantra is 'Me! Me! Me!' With the pleasure principle as its almighty master, the id doesn't just hunger for instant gratification, it demands it NOW!!!!

Although in an ideal world we'd probably all be allowed to get exactly what we want, when we want it, life is just a tad different. Sooner or later most of us are forced to come to terms with that rude awakening, that harsh painful truth, that we can't always have our appetites gratified, right there, right then. We come to realise that it's not always acceptable, appropriate or even in our own best interest to act on every urge. Our ego – which is the Latin word for 'I' – helps keep our internal toddler's temper tantrums at bay. Because the reality principle is our ego's personal rule book, its main purpose is to regulate our sexual and aggressive desires and prevent us from behaving so offensively it could lead to social purdah. Since the ego is the personality equivalent of sensible shoes and hospital corners, its mantra is likely to be: 'It's not appropriate now. You'll have to wait until later.'

The superego, which is Latin for 'over the I', is the final personality structure in psychoanalysis and acts as our moral guide. The superego houses two substructures: our conscience, which makes us feel guilty when we've done something wrong, and the ego ideal, which makes us feel good about ourselves when we've done something worthy. The superego's response to our persistent drives would be: 'Not now. Wait until you deserve it.'

According to Freud, our personality is a constant and continual struggle for dominance between the id, the ego and the superego.

Defence mechanisms

Denial, like all defence mechanisms, is an unconscious process which serves to protect us from the painful truths about ourselves, the ones which we are unwilling to face up to and address.

If we didn't have some protective psychological armour, we'd all be in a constant state of neurotic distress. According to Freud our defence mechanisms include repression, regression, rationalisation, intellectualisation, displacement, projection, reaction formation, compensation and sublimation. Each of us uses these to varying degrees. However, because they're unconscious, we are not readily aware of them.

Defence mechanisms aim to protect us from feeling undue anxiety. For example, smokers commonly refute the claims that their habit is dangerous to their health (denial). Even when confronted with the statistics on the link between smoking and lung cancer, the nicotine brigade will adamantly quote chapter and verse about how their grandparent, who smoked four packs a day, lived to be 106. Students who've failed to achieve a certain grade on an important exam have been known to complain that they were suffering from the 'flu or were excessively tired at the time of the test (rationalisation). And the downtrodden employee, unable to stand up to his bullying, aggressive boss, will frequently come home and shout at his family and kick the cat (displacement). Some men, when uncomfortable accepting their homosexual tendencies, will often go to great lengths to prove how much they detest gay people, branding them perverts and sick (reaction formation). And so on.

Criticisms

There's no doubt that during the course of his career Freud contributed greatly to our understanding of the mind and human behaviour. For my money, his main contribution was to open our eyes to the latent powers of the subconscious mind, and the importance of early-childhood relationships or attachments to parents and other carers in subsequent emotional well-being.

Although Freud's views predominated in the field of mental health for much of the last century, his influence has waned considerably over the past thirty or forty years. While Freudian psychoanalysis still remains very much shrouded in an aura of mystique, this therapeutic philosophy no longer reigns supreme as the treatment choice *du jour*. In fact, due to more recent developments and advances in psychological research, which have in turn led to further understanding of the human mind, the off-shoots of Freudian theory are far more influential these days in the fields of literature, cinema and advertising than they are within the clinician's consulting room.

Although diehard Freudians would argue that their master lived a long life and revised his theories many times, some of his seminal viewpoints now seem excessively imaginative, if not chauvinistically offensive.

Then there's the thorny question of proof – does this form of psychoanalysis actually work? – and there is a big problem here. There is very little systematic research evidence to support the more feasible tenets of psychoanalysis. For any therapy to be credible, it's first got to be observable, testable and ultimately verifiable. Defence mechanisms, the id, the ego, the superego, the Oedipus Complex, among others, are all central drives which govern our behaviour according to the canons of psychoanalysis, but because these components of the mind are unconscious processes, they prove decidedly difficult to observe and quantify with statistically valid research methodology. In other words, we don't know conclusively if Freudian psychoanalysis even works in the first place, or the extent to which its claims are true, if at all.

Behaviourism

Behaviourism was born partly out of many of the criticisms and perceived limitations of Freudian theory, and this approach is as far removed from psychoanalysis as you can possibly get – in psychological terms that is.

With its foundations rooted in the work of such scientists as Pavlov (he of the drooling dog fame) and other Russian physiologists, behaviourism based its early conclusions about human behaviour on the detailed observations of animals and their reactions to a variety of different situations.

In a nutshell, behaviourism, unlike psychoanalysis which is predicated upon unconscious, and therefore hidden, drives and impulses, is the ultimate 'show me' or 'if you can't see it, don't believe it' school of psychology. Pioneered and developed by Joseph Wolpe for application to human problems, behaviourism argues that people learn bad behaviours from their environment, and once these 'maladaptive' reactions are identified, they can therefore be unlearned.

Since its aim is to focus first on identifying unhealthy or unhelpful patterns of behaviour and their environmental triggers, rather than to resolve unconscious conflicts, behaviourism is less concerned with the deeply entrenched, traumatic origins of the problem behaviour and places its emphasis instead on the 'here and now'. So, if a child is biting other children a behavioural therapist is more interested in finding out what it is about the school's environment (teachers, boredom factors, other children) that's triggering the aggression than in exploring family relationships.

In my view, behaviourism has offered two main contributions to the field of psychology. First, its methods of studying human behaviour are observable and testable and, therefore, capable of being proven scientifically. There's a thirty- to forty-year history of research into behaviourism verifying its claims. In other words, it does what it says it does. Second, since the emphasis here is on present behaviour patterns – with the distant past left well and truly alone – the assumption is that therapy can be accomplished in a matter of weeks and months, instead of the years if not decades that psychoanalysis demands.

Behavioural therapists seek to change disturbed maladaptive behaviour patterns by applying a variety of different techniques. The most common strategies are called classical conditioning, counter conditioning, operant conditioning and social learning theory.

Classical conditioning

If our bad behaviours aren't the product of our traumatic childhood, how then are they formed? The behaviourists would argue that we are conditioned to respond in particular ways by our environment.

In classical conditioning, a particular event/object (or stimulus, to be technical) becomes somehow linked to another event/object and causes a certain response or reaction. Later, the first event/object, all on its own, may also produce the same reaction.

Here's what I mean. In the powerful cautionary novel *Brave New World*, the author Aldous Huxley depicted a future in which classical conditioning would be used to force people into rigidly narrow social categories. Some of his characters included children who were slotted into the role of workers, and therefore trained or conditioned to feel repulsion towards personal interests such as hobbies and leisure activities. In order for the futuristic oligarchy to achieve this evil goal, the children were given an electric shock (unconditioned stimulus) when faced with prohibited objects such as books or flowers (conditioned stimulus). As a result of this pairing, in just a short amount of time the children became fearful (conditioned response) whenever they were presented with any of the forbidden objects, even without the electric shock present. So, to recap, classical conditioning first begins with object + shock = the desired effect of revulsion. Then it quickly becomes object = revulsion. There's no longer any need for the shock.

In psychology there is a seminal case of classical conditioning all students of the discipline learn about. It's the famous case of 'Little Albert'.

John B. Watson was a renowned researcher who successfully conditioned this young boy to fear a white rat simply by pairing the animal with a loud noise. So, every time Little Albert saw the rat, he simultaneously heard an unpleasant bang, the sound of which caused the boy distress and terror. After only a few trials, Albert responded with distress when he saw the creature in the absence of the loud noise.

There were a few unpleasant side effects. Not only was Dr Watson so effective at creating a fear response every time Little Albert saw a rat, the young boy also became terrified when he caught sight of other furry creatures. Dogs. Cats. Even Father Christmas! Luckily, these days research studies are subjected to very tight ethical restrictions.

Counter conditioning

The goal of behavioural therapy is both to remove the stimuli that trigger maladaptive behaviours and to promote more productive, healthier reactions to these same stimuli. Counter conditioning is one weapon in the behaviourist's arsenal.

Counter conditioning is based on the theory that the body is physiologically unable to produce two opposing emotions, such as anxiety and relaxation, at the same time. Using the same principles as classical conditioning, counter conditioning aims to replace negative emotional reactions to stimuli with more positive, healthier ones.

Here's another classic example. In a study conducted in 1924 by Mary Cover Jones, a student of Dr Watson's, a three-year-old boy named Peter had developed a rabbit phobia; the origins of this fear were unknown. In order to help this little boy overcome his rabbit phobia, Jones used counter conditioning techniques. Twice a day, for a period of two months, she presented Peter with some sweets as she simultaneously brought a case containing a rabbit closer and closer to him.

Although he was initially very frightened of the animal, over the course of the study Peter became less and less afraid of the rabbit and could eventually pick it up and stroke it. The pleasant feelings associated with the sweets gradually became associated with the rabbit, leading to the dissipation (or 'extinction') of the phobia.

Operant conditioning

Behavioural therapists also use treatments called operant conditioning or behaviour modification, based on the work of the world-renowned B.F. Skinner. Popular forms of behaviour modification, which aim to change negative behavioural patterns, are predicated upon two influences: reward and punishment. The idea here is that behaviour which is immediately followed by a satisfying consequence (reward) will tend to be repeated. In contrast, behaviour which elicits an unpleasant or unwelcome reaction (punishment) is less likely to recur.

Years ago, I used to work in a child psychology department, something I loved doing. A major part of my job was teaching parenting skills and I favoured operant conditioning for many typical childhood difficulties: bedwetting, sleep disturbances, toilet training, temper tantrums, sibling rivalries, even violence. I'd often teach parents a 'star chart system' which encouraged and rewarded good behaviour while discouraging and punishing undesirable behaviour. After a thorough assessment of the presenting problematic, I'd sit down and help the family – both parents and child – work out desirable goals and a reward and punishment system to facilitate these aims. Every time the child achieved the target behaviour, he or she would be given a star. When a number were accumulated, these stars could be 'cashed in' for rewards – choosing the dessert, selecting a video, a special day out. However, should the child refuse to co-operate, stars would either be held back or taken away, rendering the desired reward out of reach.

Social learning

Another technique used by behaviourists is social learning. Think back to Mary Cover Jones' work with Peter and his rabbit phobia. When treating Peter, the scientist first encouraged the little boy to observe other children holding, stroking and playing with the rabbit. In doing so, she was employing the techniques of social learning in order for Peter to observe the desired behaviour in others. Many behavioural therapists help their clients and patients form new, positive responses and reactions by suggesting they watch and observe other people, either on tape or in person, in order to model their more adaptive, positive behaviours on them. They then try out the new behaviours themselves. Social learning is highly effective as a technique to help people overcome all kinds of personal difficulties, including phobias, developing confidence and honing social skills.

Criticisms

Although the therapy is highly effective and one of my main-choice approaches for treatment, it's not without its shortcomings. Effective though reward and punishment reinforcement may be as inducements for behavioural change, people are highly complex creatures with a whole breadth of experiences, emotions and perceptions, and therefore greater than just the sum of their constituent learned responses. In other words, this approach can be seen as too reductionist.

Person-Centred Therapy

In the fifties clinicians began to conclude that the Freudian and Pavlovian schools of therapy were doing more to raise questions about human behaviour than to provide much-needed answers. Enter Carl Rogers with his particular brand of person-centred therapy (PCT), once called client-centred therapy (CCT). Sometimes referred to as the 'third force', to distinguish itself from psychoanalysis and behaviourism, PCT is a huge departure from these earlier traditions.

Carl Rogers held an entirely different view of people and the formation of their problems from his therapeutic predecessors. PCT is the ultimate 'love the sinner, hate the sin' therapy and its central tenet stems from the conviction that every person is essentially, innately good and well-meaning.

In this therapeutic framework, psychological distress and problems are thought to occur due to a discrepancy between a person's public self and his/her true self. The tension caused by these duelling, clashing selves leads the individual to distort reality or deny his or her feelings in a vain attempt to avoid the inevitable anxiety or distress. The therapist's aim, therefore, is to help the client achieve self-actualisation. Once the individual resolves this inner conflict and becomes his or her true self, the tensions and anxieties consequently fade away.

The goal of PCT is, therefore, first to promote self-acceptance and then to facilitate the individual's pursuit of self-actualisation. However, the therapist isn't expected to offer expertise or guidance. PCT is a non-directive kind of therapy. In other words, doling out pearls of wisdom or offering concrete advice to clients on their problems is verboten. Because, as Rogers argued, we all possess our own innate ability to solve our own problems, a therapist's role here is to encourage the client to come up with his or her own solutions. This is achieved through clinician empathy, active listening and unconditional positive regard (the love the sinner, hate the sin part). Once this stage is set, the clinician then helps the client explore their true inner emotions about their current situation and their aspired goals through a process called reflection of feelings.

Criticisms

Because of its then revolutionary warm and feel-good view of people and their problems, it's little wonder that PCT, particularly in the seventies, once dominated the therapeutic world. It's still widely popular today, and without a doubt this approach has a number of clinical strengths. For example, we can thank Carl Rogers for pioneering the concept of providing a client with a safe, trusting, open environment in which to explore their thoughts and feelings without fear of disapproval or judgement – aspects of clinical practice previously unheard of or ignored in the realms of psychoanalysis and behaviourism.

However, PCT is far from being the perfect therapy. Its policies and practices of empathy and active listening are valid, but often insufficient to help people overcome their problems. Clinical psychologists like myself aim to incorporate these techniques into more specialised treatments like CBT, psychoanalysis, and sometimes even behaviourism.

In addition, the non-directive nature of PCT, hailed as its strength, is in my view more often a limitation. The therapist's incessant 'So-what-do-you-think? How-do-you-feel?' style of reflective questioning can easily turn into aimlessness and lead to client frustration. Sometimes, clients want guidance, advice and direction with their problems, and complain that if they already knew what they thought and how they felt, they wouldn't need to come to a therapist.

PCT on its own is not appropriate for every psychological problem. Evidence has not been forthcoming to support this therapy choice for treating anxiety, phobias, eating disorders, obsessive-compulsive disorder, addictions or depression. In fact, when people are depressed, one of the cardinal symptoms of the disorder is excessive rumination or thought-dwelling. Since PCT actively encourages people to reflect on their feelings and thinking, the therapy can end up making depressed clients feel more trapped in their endless cycle of despair.

Finally, it's very hard for a therapist to maintain a passive, non-directive, reflective stance as required in the PCT tradition, especially if clients demonstrate little insight into their own thoughts, feelings and personal problems.

Cognitive Therapy

And . . . finally . . . cognitive therapy.

Once upon a time, in the first century AD, there lived a Greek Stoic philosopher called Epictetus. People who were highly irrational, he observed, often had a greater predilection for emotional distress.

A few centuries later, in *Hamlet*, Shakespeare penned the lines: 'There's nothing either good or bad, but thinking makes it so'.

In other words, Epictetus and Hamlet could be seen as early proponents of cognitive therapy. Several centuries later, the psychoanalyst Alfred Adler claimed 'meanings are not determined by situations, but we determine ourselves by the meanings we *give* situations'. These very diverse sources sum up the core philosophy of cognitive therapy.

It was first devised by Albert Ellis, an erstwhile psychoanalytic psychotherapist, and Aaron Beck, a psychiatrist, although each developed slightly different versions of the school. Cognitive therapy in its pure form first entered the clinical arena in the late-sixties. As noted before, this therapeutic paradigm now far eclipses all other approaches to treatment and is the predominant tradition of choice for clinicians all around the world.

How does cognitive therapy differ from all others? Why has it proven so influential? Throughout this book we'll be looking at all the ins and outs of our thinking patterns and the ways in which they impinge on our emotions, our physical well-being and our behaviours. However, simply put, cognitive therapists have formed three main conclusions unique from previous psychological traditions.

As the name suggests, in CBT cognitions, beliefs and thought processes are deemed central to personal difficulties, but theorists also argue that our social environment, physical feelings and behaviours are all inextricably linked. If one of these areas is affected in some way, it's pretty much guaranteed that the others will be affected too.

Secondly, the focus is on the subjectivity of our experiences. More specifically, cognitive clinicians would argue that events, circumstances or situations, however stressful and even traumatic they may be to us, are not the true cause of our emotional distress or troubled behaviours. It is our *interpretation* of these events that leads to problems.

Thirdly, in interpreting the meaning of stressful events, we regularly engage in something called 'faulty thinking', or 'irrational logic' in CBT language, and it's this brand of sophistry which is the real key to our anxiety and distress. In other words, people in distress often tend to reach the wrong conclusions, often the most personally disastrous and self-defeating ones at that, which only reinforces and exacerbates their misery.

So in CBT our personal situations, feelings, thoughts, physical sensations and behaviours are all intertwined. And our emotional responses to a situation, such as an argument with our partner or a failed job interview, are determined not by the incident itself, but by our subjective and, therefore, unique interpretation of the event (such as possible fears of abandonment or feelings of hopelessness).

Here's an example. Three different men are going for a job interview. Each has been out of work for a long time and is desperate for the job. They all want to clinch this position so badly they can taste it.

As each leaves his house and heads to company headquarters, suddenly, without warning, the skies open up and it begins to bucket down with rain. Since the weatherman has predicted sunshine that day, this sudden downpour is completely unexpected. Without umbrellas, they all became soaked to the skin. How does each man respond?

The first becomes very negative and pessimistic. 'Look at me, I'm a mess. I knew something really terrible would happen. I just knew it,' he curses. 'I can never, ever get ahead. Every time I try to do something positive with my life, I just get it thrown straight back in my face. There's no point in going to the interview now – they'll only laugh at me anyway. And who can blame them? I'm such a loser.'

The second man doesn't fare too well either, but his reaction is different. He's so upset about his waterlogged appearance, he starts to panic so badly that beads of cold sweat break out on his forehead and pour down his face. His heart starts pounding uncontrollably; so much so, he convinces himself he's having a heart attack and heads for the nearest casualty department. All thoughts of the interview are immediately abandoned.

The final man reacts with optimism. He's just glad it was rain. It could have been much worse. It could have been a flock of pigeons!

See, same situation, three different interpretations.

The A-B-Cs of CBT

Since our thoughts are seen as central to our feelings, physical well-being and actions, the aim of cognitive behavioural therapy is, therefore, to help people improve their lives by making constructive and positive changes to their thinking strategies, perceptions and beliefs. Therapists first teach their clients to identify the problem areas they'd like to work on and then help them become aware of the faulty thinking that underlies their personal issues. Once difficulties are brought into the open, the therapist normally teaches the clients the tools and techniques to challenge their self-defeating beliefs and replace them with more rational, balanced attitudes.

Cognitive behavioural therapy usually comes to an end once we are taught the skills to perceive ourselves, others and the world around us in a healthier light, because it follows that other areas in our lives – our feelings, physical well-being and behaviours – will improve as a result.

Version 1: Rational-Emotive Therapy (R-E-T) or Rational-Emotive-Behaviour Therapy (R-E-B-T)

There are two main schools of CBT, devised by Albert Ellis and Aaron Beck, the pioneers of this method. While the basic themes are pretty much the same, there are still some striking differences between them and I'd like you to become familiar with both interpretations. Throughout this book, you'll be learning to look at and analyse your life the CBT way. At some points, when you're facing a particular dilemma, you might find Ellis' approach more helpful. In others, Beck's will help provide the answers.

Dr Ellis is probably one of the most renowned and venerated psychologists on the planet today. His version of CBT was born out of his frustrations with the limitations of psychoanalysis.

Although initially schooled in the Freudian psychoanalytic tradition himself, he eventually became disenchanted with this therapy, finding it misguided and claiming the Viennese psychiatrist 'got sidetracked into people's early childhood, their lusting after their parents and their deeply unconscious hatreds and guilts'. Ellis felt that placing the emphasis on such matters was only a red herring where emotional well-being was concerned. In his view, the true barriers to present happiness are not damaging influences endured as children. Rather, present obstacles to achieving our dreams are very much the product of our own self-imposed, unrealistic expectations about ourselves and the world around us.

Rational-Emotive Therapy (or Rational-Emotive-Behavioural Therapy) is a type of cognitive therapy developed by Dr Ellis to help people alter what he refers to as irrational beliefs that take hold of their lives, other people and the world around them. Because our emotions, thoughts and behaviours are inextricably linked together, this therapy uses the A-B-C theory of emotion, in which A represents some activating event, circumstance or situation, B is an irrational belief, thought or perception that is triggered by the event, and C reflects the emotional consequence. According to Ellis, most people erroneously believe it's A that causes C, when in fact it's B that causes C.

Here's how Ellis' R-E-B-T works. Imagine that you've just found out you've failed an important exam (A), and you feel gutted and worried as a result (C). Ellis would argue that your negative feelings are not due to your poor test score, but to the irrational belief (B) that you must be perfect. So, it's the view you hold of yourself and your need to strive for perfection that lets you down, not the low grade.

R-E-B-T and R-E-T therapists help their clients first identify their irrational beliefs and then set about challenging them. They will ask for evidence in support of these beliefs and then set out to contradict and poke holes in these faulty thoughts.

Here's a verbatim copy of a transcript illustrating the methods an R-E-T therapist (T) uses to challenge a client's (C) irrational beliefs. The client is a twenty-one-year-old male who is experiencing feelings of guilt because he believes he hasn't lived up to his parents' high expectations.

C: It was always this way. If I didn't do well in school or even in a particular test if I didn't do as well as I wanted to.

T: I see. So you used to blame yourself? Beat yourself up over it?

C: Yes.

T: But why? What's the use of doing that? Are you supposed to be perfect? Why the hell shouldn't human beings make mistakes. None of us is perfect.

C: But you have to be perfect in this world.

T: Yes. But is that rational?

C: No.

T: Why do it? Why not give up that unrealistic expectation?

C: But then I can't accept myself.

T: But you're saying, 'It's not acceptable to make mistakes.' It is human to make mistakes. That is how we learn.

C: I want their approval – my parents approval. I want them to be proud.

T: Yes, that's part of it. But don't you see. You're saying they'll love me and be proud of me only if I don't make mistakes. Your parents might be upset, might be let down, but that's different from not loving you

Albert Ellis' approach to therapy is often criticised for being hard-hitting and blunt at times, as this transcript clearly demonstrates, so it's not always for the faint of heart. However, this bold, harsh, Socratic style is justified, according to Ellis, in order to challenge deeply held and enduring irrational beliefs. Because these faulty perceptions are automatic, unconscious and deeply entrenched in our cognitive and emotional make-up, they can be stubbornly persistent. This said, not all R-E-T/R-E-B-T therapists adopt this hard-line view and many aim to 'soften the blow' and provide the warmth and empathy advocated by Carl Rogers.

Version 2: Beck's Cognitive Therapy

Dr Aaron Beck's version of cognitive therapy, which is more clinically widespread than that of Dr Ellis and more akin to my own personal and professional tastes, has a slightly different focus. Originating from his work with people suffering from clinical depression, Dr Beck's version is predicated upon the view that negative beliefs about oneself, the world and the future are at the heart of our distress. Based on his clinical observations, Dr Beck came to note that distressed or unhappy people tend mainly:

1. to blame themselves rather than their circumstances for their misfortunes;
2. to focus much more on negative events and situations, to filter out their positive ones;
3. and to hold pessimistic, bleak views of the future.

But it doesn't just stop there. The problem is our disabling thought processes have a niggling, persistent tendency to worsen our existing bleak mood, which in turn breeds further unhappiness. And so on. I call this cycle of negative thinking and despair 'thought spiralling'.

Sometimes, this bleak thought-emotions entanglement gets so out of control, people lose all sense of perspective and dire consequences occur. I was reading the newspaper the other day and came across a very tragic story that exemplifies this point. A young woman studying to be a lawyer had just completed her final exams.

As she waited for her test results, she began to panic and, as the hours wore on, became increasingly anxious that her marks wouldn't be high enough to secure the glittering legal job she wanted. This in turn bred destructively negative thinking patterns. So much so that one day, when she couldn't stand the tension any longer, she rushed over to the law faculty and held a cleaner up at gunpoint to get hold of a set of keys to the main office. She barged in and set about frantically searching the place for her results. Unfortunately, once she'd prised open the filing cabinet and found her marks, the news was not good. They were a little lower than she'd hoped for. With her panic levels through the ceiling by this point, she decided to falsify them to reflect a higher, more desirable level.

Predictably, the benighted law student was caught. Within a matter of a day or so, the authorities had discovered the altered results and confronted her with the evidence. Ashamed and humiliated by her behaviour, this woman took her own life soon after.

Luckily, stories like this are extremely rare, but they illustrate an important CBT point about human nature, feelings and perceptions. When our thoughts and emotions spin out of control, our ability to reason or consider alternative options clearly flies straight out of the window. If this distressed young woman had maintained a calm, rational frame of mind, it is unlikely that she would have taken the extreme measure of committing suicide. I'm not saying she wouldn't be disappointed, even gutted, but she would have been able to analyse the situation more logically. She might have been able to explore other options, find out about the possibility of retakes. She might have discovered her future employers were less concerned about her marks than she had feared and would offer her the job anyway. And no doubt countless other options could have been considered. The point is that when we're distressed, anxious or upset, our brains just don't, can't, won't engage logically. No matter how hard we try. We end up torturing ourselves and our behaviour gets out of control.

If this young law student had been a client of Aaron Beck's, his version of cognitive therapy would have aimed to break this cycle and promote happier, healthier living by helping her first identify and then change her distorted, negative beliefs – about herself, her perceived failure, her future – powerful and pervasive as they might seem.

In his treatment approach, Beck's style is less forceful and hard-hitting than that of Ellis, although he also employs a direct, Socratic technique in order to help people recognise and challenge their irrational belief systems. In order to do so, Beck would normally require his clients and patients to keep a daily diary of their thoughts, particularly in connection with specific situations or circumstances that trigger strong emotional reactions, and encourage them to identify the specific thoughts linked to these strong feelings. His ultimate goal is to help the client replace these negative, destructive emotions with positive, constructive, more balanced ones.

Here's a familiar example, similar to that we used in R-E-T. A client who's been achieving poor marks, feels down about his abilities, discouraged that he's destined only to be a failure in life and tempted to drop out of his course, would be encouraged to analyse the situation differently. Probably something like this. 'If I work harder and change my study habits, then I'll be able to improve my academic performance. If my marks improve, then I will graduate and be able to strive for the career I want.'

To promote positive experiences, Beck usually gives his clients homework assignments and tasks (the behavioural part) to help reinforce the development of these rational beliefs.

EVALUATING CBT

As you now more fully appreciate, CBT differs in many respects from other traditional schools of psychological therapy. Its strengths and widespread clinical influence seem to stem mainly from the fact that Ellis and Beck learned from many of the limitations and shortcomings of their therapeutic predecessors. CBT is a sort of 'new and improved' psychology, if you will. And these improvements are its incredible strengths.

Unlike psychoanalysis, for example, CBT is a short-term therapy, usually lasting only for about eight to ten sessions, and emphasises the 'here and now'. Because it stresses our conscious thought processes, it foregoes the temptation to trawl the murky nether regions of the subconscious. And, unlike psychoanalysis, CBT has been the subject of countless valid research studies and has a proven track record of effectiveness.

Unlike behaviourism, CBT believes that our environment is influential upon but insufficient on its own to explain psychological unhappiness, and aims to tease out the irrational beliefs and faulty thinking strategies that underlie and govern our behaviours and emotions, replacing them with more balanced thought biases.

CBT is an active therapy which focuses on helping people develop problem-solving skills and equipping them with the tools and techniques to live happier, healthier lives.

Finally, unlike all its predecessors, which breed a sense of dependence on therapists, CBT encourages people to become their own shrink. It teaches all the skills necessary to analyse, identify and overcome personal difficulties and problems. For all these reasons and more, CBT is the ultimate self-help therapy.

Criticisms

CBT offers people a huge number of benefits and when its techniques are put into practice, they really transform our beliefs about ourselves, our abilities, our expectations and the world around us.

A lot of critics, however, have argued that CBT can be a bit harsh, insensitive, even brutal. There are also rumblings afoot that the techniques and methods can be too intellectually demanding for the majority of people.

Is there any truth in these accusations? Well, yes and no. Although Albert Ellis adopts a short sharp shock kind of approach when working with his clients, many CBT therapists don't. I don't. In terms of intellectual requirements, I have used CBT techniques with people with learning disabilities, children and adults with dementia. So, in my view, for CBT to be effective, it's down to the skill and the personal style of the therapist.

Some of my clients ask me if, since situations trigger upsetting thoughts and feelings, it wouldn't be easier just to change said situations. Find a new job. Advertise for a new roommate. End a relationship. Drop a degree course.

I make two points in rebuttal. As you know, sometimes our thoughts and feelings conspire to spiral out of control, so that our interpretation of a situation is often worse than the reality. Also, not only can major changes like these be drastic, but merely changing your circumstances without really analysing why they pose such specific difficulties for you, can lead to similar disasters occurring. There's no automatic guarantee that the new job, roommate, relationship or career alternative will be any better than its predecessor. Unless your environment is unsafe in some way or that you're putting up with what I call the three intolerable and dangerous As from people in your life – abuse, affairs or addictions – for which you must seek immediate help, then CBT is a good first port of call for problem-solving.

With these points in mind, however, I do have two quibbles with the traditional theoretical premises of CBT. The first has to do with the centrality of the thought processes in determining our well-being. Many CBT therapists have argued that negative thoughts cause psychological disturbances, particularly depression, but I disagree. I have researched the field of mood disorders extensively, for example, and have written for scientists, researchers and clinicians, and have found no evidence anywhere for these claims. Emotional distress, negative thinking, physical symptoms and behaviours all go hand in hand. In my view, negative thoughts reflect the symptoms of many psychological disorders; they are not the causes of them. In fact, we still don't fully understand the origins of psychological difficulties, so this widespread assumption about the central role of beliefs is to my mind misleading.

Second, even though CBT has radically revolutionised treatment practices, I do not believe that the other, previous schools of therapy are redundant and I draw on the best elements from each in my professional practice. From psychoanalysis, I believe our childhood and personal histories have a huge impact on our lives: the way we feel, how we behave. Although CBT stresses the here and now, we can't discard the influence of our past entirely.

From behaviourism, I borrow the scientific, observational paradigm. I always set my clients homework tasks and assignments and encourage them to perform behaviour experiments.

Although Carl Rogers' approach to therapy is too non-interventionist on its own for my tastes, I agree it is crucial that people should feel comfortable, trusting and able openly to discuss their thoughts, worries and concerns with the therapist.

MY CBT PROGRAM FOR PERSONAL HAPPINESS

The aim of this nine-week program is to help you develop a greater sense of emotional well-being and contentment. It's designed for everyone who wants to feel better about themselves and their circumstances. This book is not designed to replace a qualified therapist or intended for people with severe symptoms of psychological distress. If your problems are proving insurmountable or difficult to handle, then please make an appointment with your doctor immediately.

From the CBT paradigm, I will teach you all the necessary skills to help you identify, address and counterbalance the irrational beliefs and faulty thoughts that lead to discontentment, low self-esteem, lack of confidence and other symptoms of unhappiness. Also, as our personal situations, our emotions, our behaviours and our physical state are all interconnected, it's important that we look to improve these essential areas of our life as well. Working towards this goal, I draw heavily on the scientific research on happiness and subjective well-being, including the works of Michael Eysenck, Robert Holden, Michael Argyle and others.

Here's what you can expect to achieve from your study of *Wearing the Ruby Slippers*:

Greater happiness and overall emotional well-being
Better physical fitness
Problem-solving skills
Greater sense of control over your life, at work and in your
    relationships
Become more adept at coping with unforeseen difficulties and
    disasters
More confidence
Personal fulfilment

Lions and tigers and bears, oh my!

Here's the catch. You will have to put in your fair share of effort. After all, just about everything we do to improve our lot in life comes at a cost. Everything worthwhile, that is. A good education. A prestigious career. Athletic skill. The same goes for achieving happiness.

Time investment

You'll have to set aside some time. This program is nine weeks in duration. During this period, I'll be asking you to complete lots of different exercises and tasks. Since I believe people learn more effectively through doing, rather than just from reading, time commitment is an important factor. So you might want to think about prioritising current commitments, and giving up some of your free time. I suspect that ultimately you'll find the investment required a small price to pay.

Commitment to the program

Couch potatoes, be warned! In order to gain maximum benefit from this program, you'll have to be genuinely motivated and concentrate your mind on the reading and exercises. If you just go through the motions or half-heartedly follow the tasks or occasionally pick up the book in between ferrying your kids to school and the dog to the vet, then you won't really benefit.

Be patient

You probably won't notice any major improvements in your mood for a few weeks, because the benefits of these exercises are cumulative. They are designed to work in conjunction with one another. So don't expect instant results.

Breaking free from your comfort zone

Throughout the nine weeks, you'll be gaining new insights into yourself and developing a whole new set of skills. In fact, your personal self-discoveries will be a major source of enrichment and fun during the course. However, whenever we venture out into unfamiliar territory, learn new skills, try different patterns of behaviour, the novelty of these situations can breed a little anxiety. Any time we break free from our comfort zones, even those that make us feel unhappy or stifled, we're entering into new, uncharted ground and leaving our safe havens behind. The exercises and tasks I've included here may seem a little eccentric at times, but most people really enjoy them and find them rewarding.

You may feel bad before you feel better

At some point during the course, you might feel a little over-whelmed by thoughts and feelings that emerge. Mostly these negative reactions, or abreactions, are a release of pent-up emotions and the effect will be cathartic. Sometimes, however, especially for people who bury their feelings, just the mere experience of emotion alone is new and unsettling.

As you proceed with this course, you will gain deeper insight into these reactions and will become more equipped to handle them. However, if at any point along the way you start to feel confused or unduly upset about any personal revelations that emerge, then please, seek help from your doctor immediately.

CBT RECAP

The techniques are easy to learn, easy to apply

Originally designed to help people with psychological distress, its techniques are applicable to everyone and the personal difficulties they face

CBT focuses on the here and now, so it's not always necessary to look for hidden, unconscious traumas to resolve our problems

There are five components to any problem: environment, physical sensations, emotions, behaviours and thoughts

Each of the five components affects and interacts with the others

Small changes in one area can lead to changes in the others

Identifying the five components of your own difficulties can help target areas for change

People are taught coping skills and strategies to address their own problems and become their own 'therapist'

Improvements happen very quickly

I think that's enough for an introduction. Before you start the program I'd like you to take some time to think about how your thoughts, feelings, social situations and physical symptoms are all interconnected. Buy yourself an exercise book and write this down. When have you been at your happiest? When have you been at your unhappiest? Can you identify any situations, thoughts, physical sensations or behaviours associated with these experiences? When you've done this, you're ready to begin.

The Meaning of Happiness

Welcome to the first week of the program. Over the past few days, you've been given the chance to appraise your life and think about the times when you've been at your happiest and those occasions when you've been at your lowest ebb. Were you able to tease out the different thoughts, emotions, physical feelings and behaviours which were linked to each occasion? If you have, well done. Identifying these different facets and factors isn't always easy, but they are the building blocks of CBT. If you found the task difficult, don't worry. Remember, we're just at the start of the program and there'll be plenty of opportunities along the way for you to fine-tune and develop these skills.

The overriding theme of this week is understanding happiness. With CBT, we spend a lot of time conceiving and achieving goals. And, before you can actually go out and get what you want, in this case happiness, you first have to have a clear grasp of the concept's meaning. It might already seem blatantly obvious to you what happiness is, but I argue that if we all already knew what it was, there wouldn't be a need for books like this one. Read on.

Listed below are your tasks for this week to help you understand how happiness may be defined.

1. Life Priorities Exercise
2. Reasons to be Happy Exercise
3. Meaning of Happiness Exercise
4. Emotional Intensity Quiz
5. Happiness Questionnaire

EXERCISE 1:
WHAT ARE YOUR PRIORITIES IN LIFE?

Let's jump straight in and look at your personal attitudes towards happiness. The aim of this task is to help you clarify what's important to you in life. So, grab a pen and a notebook and find a quiet place where you'll be left in peace for about five or ten minutes.

Now, I'd like you to brainstorm ideas to the following question: what are your requirements for a personally satisfying life?

Write down as many answers as you'd like. People I work with often come up with as few as three, but sometimes as many as ten or even twenty. Don't get bogged down by worrying about correct or incorrect responses – there are none. Don't fret about complete sentences, key words or phrases will do. This task is about you and unearthing your personal thoughts and feelings, so however you choose to do it is fine.

Remember, too, since this is a brainstorming exercise, I want you to jot down everything that springs to mind in relation to this question. You don't have to take too long. Three or four minutes will suffice. But, just in case you get stuck, many people write down such topics as relationships, career, travel, feelings, material possessions, their values, health and education, but the list is virtually endless.

Once you're satisfied that you've included your main priorities on your list, I then want you to return to the items and rate each one separately in terms of importance. I suggest a five-point scale, where five represents all those items which are most important and valuable to you and, at the other end of the scale, one signifies the least important goals and ambitions. Those it would be great to have, but when push comes to shove, you can live without. The twos, threes and fours fall somewhere in between. Once you've done that, group all the items together by number value, so that all the fives will be together, the fours, the threes and so on.

Now, the sixty-four-thousand-dollar questions. Where did happiness appear on your list? Is your sense of personal satisfaction more important to you than your career, for example? Or is it, perhaps, less important than your relationship with your partner? Are certain items linked in your mind with happiness? Was it at the top or bottom of your list? What does its position say to you? Did happiness even appear on your list at all? If not, why not?

If you ranked it highly, then that's great. If not, don't worry. We're now going to look at the things holding you back from achieving a happy life.

EXERCISE 2:
REASONS TO BE HAPPY – NOT!

Ian Dury and the Blockheads once listed their reasons to be cheerful, but in my experience people generally tend not to count their blessings. Instead, they usually come up with a whole litany of explanations defending their right to be miserable. For people who set a high value on personal satisfaction, I know this negative attitude may seem hard to believe. But I can truly understand the reasons many balk at the suggestion of striving for happiness. It's because happiness, more often than not, gets a very bad press.

I experience this bad press myself. When I tell my colleagues, friends and acquaintances that I'm writing on the subject of happiness, they tend to raise a sceptical eyebrow.

For some reason, psychological subjects are often only deemed credible and worthwhile if they focus on misery and distress. Psychologists are the original doomsayers. I recently conducted a literature search and found: 70,000 studies on depression, 60,000 on stress, 51,000 on anxiety, 14,000 on aggression, and only 3,000 on happiness. So, if the very people who work in the field of emotional well-being dismiss happiness as being somehow frivolous and silly, it's not so surprising that negative beliefs flourish among the general public.

Before we can go any further, we need to look at your own personal reservations. Unless these obstacles or lingering doubts are confronted now, they'll only keep cropping up and getting in the way. So, time for another short exercise. Here, I want you to take about three or four minutes and write down all the reasons why you can't or shouldn't aim for happiness. Again, as with the first exercise, this task aims to tap into your thoughts and your feelings, so there's no need to worry about right or wrong answers. There aren't any.

Here's what other people commonly say on the subject:

'I might look silly.'

'It's too self-indulgent and selfish.'

'Happiness is impossible to achieve, so why try?'

'I'll just get my hopes raised, only for them to be dashed.'

'I'll fail miserably and end up feeling worse than ever before.'

'It's too much like hard work.'

'It sounds too good to be true.'

'It's naive to strive for happiness.'

'What's the point? It won't last anyway.'

'Happiness is a frivolous pursuit.'

'I just know that as soon as I become happy, it will all be snatched away.'

'I don't really like change.'

'I'm not capable of feeling happy.'

'I'm afraid to try.'

'I don't have the time.'

'How is it possible to find happiness in this day and age?'

Even though myths and prejudices about striving for happiness abound, and although they can be powerful and persuasive, this doesn't mean they're automatically true or valid. In fact, just the opposite. The psychological research actually demonstrates that being happy, far from being pointless or frivolous, is enormously beneficial to us, our health and well-being. Still not convinced? Read on.

DON'T WORRY, BE HAPPY. HERE'S WHY

Reason to be cheerful 1: Heaven's got enough martyrs

The eminent psychologist Dr Albert Ellis and his colleague Dr Irving Becker said it best when asked to defend our right to achieve happiness: 'You damn' well better! If you don't achieve your desires, your goals, your values, who will get them for you?'

Some people do insist it's wrong and selfish to put their aims and ambitions first. Wouldn't the world be a much better place if we all sacrificed our needs for those of others? In theory, I wholeheartedly agree with this view. But is it realistic?

Albert Ellis has observed that even the most altruistic of souls are not actually quite as selfless as they seem. There's usually some hidden personal agenda. Some crave an elevated sense of self-worth by helping other people. In other cases, it's the implicit expectation of gratitude or the assumption that catering to every whim and wish of others will make them more likeable or lovable.

So, as the seemingly misanthropic psychological research shows, self-sacrificing behaviour doesn't tend to win the hearts and minds of others. Often just the reverse. While there may well be many people in your life who appreciate your generosity and your caring efforts, others may see these traits as an opportunity to exploit and use you. You'll end up feeling like a doormat and your self-esteem will plummet.

If you're always the designated shoulder to cry on or the first port of call in a crisis, you have to be careful. If people are accustomed to seeing you as their Rock of Gibraltar, they are likely to become anxious and distressed themselves if the tables are turned.

I am not suggesting you become cold-hearted. The world would be a pretty grim place if we all turned our backs on other people in their time of need. I am advising, however, that you value and consider your own needs, too.

Reason to be cheerful 2: You'll be a social butterfly

Laugh and the world laughs with you, cry and you cry alone. Misery only loves company when unhappy people want to drag others down to their gloomy level. Happiness, on the other hand, is infectious, magnetic and enormously appealing. When you're genuinely happy, you'll automatically relate better to those around you. And, in turn, people will be drawn to you.

Two renowned experts in the field of happiness, Ed Diener and Martin Seligman, recently published a study they conducted on 222 participants. They divided these willing subjects into three categories in terms of happiness: highly happy, average and below average, and investigated personality types, social relations, romantic relations, physical exercise and mental health issues.

The end result? It pays dividends and beyond to be 'highly happy'. These venerated researchers found that such people were much more likely to enjoy a full social life, be lucky in love, and to spend less time alone. As if a rich social and personal life weren't enough, the highly happy also benefited from outgoing and pleasant personalities and were much less neurotic than their less happy counterparts.

So were they just lucky and blessed? No, according to the study. The fates hadn't dealt the highly happy any more 'objectively defined good events in their life', and they also experienced the occasional bad day. What do you think the CBT rationale might be for explaining these results? How about differences in subjective interpretation of events for a start?

Reason to be cheerful 3: You'll be the picture of health

Happiness makes us healthy. A recent study conducted by New York psychologist Arthur Stone found that a regular cocktail of enjoyable events boosts and strengthens our immune system. What's more, the positive effect generated by a pleasant social encounter will last for several days. In sharp contrast, however, events that are unpleasant and stressful impair our immune system, leaving us more vulnerable to infectious illness.

If a healthier life fails to convince you, how about a longer life? Being happy adds years to our longevity. In the seventies, a team of researchers conducted a nine-year investigation with 7,000 people and looked at the impact of happiness and close social ties on physical health. The results were astounding. At the end of the research period, ninety percent of 'happy, social' men and women were still alive, compared with only thirty percent of 'unhappy loners'. According to these investigators, the participants with few close relationships were less inclined to look after their health and tended to smoke, drink and lead sedentary lifestyles.

Reason to be cheerful 4: Your self-image will soar

When we're happy, we have more confidence and rate ourselves more highly. Our elevated self-esteem, in turn, has a beneficial impact on the way we interact with the world.

Unhappy people, by contrast, peer at the world through blue-tinted glasses and insist gloomily that every silver lining has a dark cloud lurking around somewhere. These people will be hyper-critical and only find flaws in themselves, their situations and others.

Reason to be cheerful 5: Move over, Einstein

Okay, so being happy may not automatically make you eligible for Mensa or guarantee you a Nobel Prize, but studies have shown that feeling good within yourself will improve your intellectual abilities. Compared to sad men and women, happy individuals think much more quickly, come up with more satisfactory solutions, avoid getting side-tracked or stuck for an answer, and are more creative.

Reason to be cheerful 6: You'll cope better

When people are unhappy, they often resort to all kinds of unhealthy or unhelpful strategies to combat or anaesthetise their low mood. Excessive eating, shopping, drugs, alcohol, smoking, exercise, inappropriate sexual liaisons, workaholic tendencies: you name it, they all block out pain. However, they're not real solutions. They're temporary distractions and make people feel much worse in the long run. Debt, drug addiction, alcohol dependency, job burnout, weight gain, respiratory ailments, guilt. Need I say more?

And the final reason . . .

I'm sure you'll agree that these are some pretty compelling reasons why the search for happiness is not a frivolous, selfish, pointless pursuit; in fact, it's just the opposite. You'll be healthier, more confident, more creative and more popular. As long as your happiness isn't contingent upon hurting yourself or harming others, then what's stopping you?

DEFINING HAPPINESS

If I asked you to define happiness you might think it's so self-evident, so obvious, that there's little point in taking the time to discuss the concept any further. Surely just about everyone knows what happiness is? Well, yes and no. We've all experienced being happy at some point in our lives – when we've fallen in love, passed an exam, travelled on the holiday of a lifetime, or got married, for example. And we've witnessed joy and elation in our friends and family. However, while it's tempting to believe that what's true for us is equally true for others, anecdotal experiences of happiness alone don't automatically qualify us as experts in the field. What we need instead is empirical, or scientific, explanations and we find those in the psychological research.

EXERCISE 3:
WHAT DOES HAPPINESS MEAN TO YOU?

If you were given the task of defining happiness, what would you come up with? Perhaps you'd equate it with an end-goal as in 'I'll be happy when I finish my degree' or 'I'll be thrilled when I lose ten pounds'? Or maybe in your view being happy is caused by a personal circumstance such as falling in love? Or could it be dependent on having an optimistic frame of mind? Perhaps you think that some people are just born with naturally sunny personalities? Or maybe you think it's all down to luck shining favourably in your direction? Could it be purely physical – a smile on your face and a bounce in your step? Is it all of the above? Some of the above?

The concept of happiness is open to wide interpretation, so before we can even begin to think about achieving this goal, it's a good idea first to clarify what we mean. Let's start by looking at what happiness *isn't*.

The myths about happiness (or what happiness ISN'T)

1. **Happiness and unhappiness are NOT two sides of the same coin.** Happiness and unhappiness are two separate and distinct processes. In other words, we're not automatically going to feel happy just because we don't feel unhappy. Instead, we're quite capable of filling that emotional void with other emotions such as boredom, fear, guilt, anger, anxiety or disappointment, among others. The moral of this story is, therefore, there's no guarantee that happiness will happen on its own. That's why we need to take active steps to achieve this goal.

2. **Happiness is NOT synonymous with pleasure.** Although we often associate happiness with sensations of pleasure, we mustn't

confuse hedonistic physical feelings with happiness. The buzz we feel, whether from drugs, shopping, nicotine, excessive exercise, overeating, is only temporary and wears off very quickly. Ironically, the buzz often even increases our feelings of dissatisfaction when our mood levels return to normal.

3. **Happiness is NOT a rose-tinted attitude towards life.** Happiness is not a positive attitude. Looking on the bright side of a bleak situation and searching for the cloud's silver lining are to be encouraged *only* if people first accept and work with their negative emotions. Unpleasant feelings, undesirable as they may be, are normal reactions to personal catastrophes and must be acknowledged. Denying their existence, ignoring them or downplaying their impact will only lead to frustration and despair.

There's a wonderfully funny character from the TV series *Marion and Geoff* whose pastiche of this denial tendency is just right. His name is Keith and he's a Welsh cab-driver. Everything goes wrong in his life, but his tenacious optimism cannot be dented. In the opening episode Keith finds out his wife has left him for another man. Does our hero rant and rave in despair? Does he grieve for his loss? Does he feel the pain of rejection? No. Keith's pathologically perky reaction is: 'I haven't lost a wife, I've gained a new best friend!'

People sometimes feel *forced* to put on a brave face in times of adversity and, in my clinical practice, I all the time hear trite sentiments like 'whatever doesn't kill us, doc, makes us stronger'. Actually, not always. Often life's emotional car crashes can leave us feeling traumatised, victimised and abused. Putting on a brave face, keeping our chin up, looking at that half-full glass, might be putting on a good show for others, but it almost certainly guarantees the perpetuation of our misery.

4. **Happiness is NOT the opposite of clinical depression.** There is a myth that clinical depression is synonymous with sadness, and that both are the opposite of happiness. Wrong. When people commonly talk of depression they're usually referring to the extreme feelings of sadness following a negative life event such as bereavement, sudden unemployment, or a relationship breakdown. Strong, profound, even unbearable degrees of sadness and pain are, as I've said, normal reactions to personal loss. Clinical depression, on the other hand, is not a reaction to an upsetting situation. It's an illness, albeit one characterised most often by emotional symptoms, that develops out of the blue. In other words, if people can link their feelings of depression to a stressful event, chances are it's profound sadness they're experiencing. If they can't trace their symptoms to a loss or major life upheaval, then biological depression is likely to be the culprit.

5. **Happiness is NOT a particular personality trait.** Although we can all name people blessed with sunny, cheerful dispositions, it's an oversimplification to equate solely personality with happiness. While there are some rare individuals diagnosed with a form of depression called dysthymia, who are chronically unhappy, most other people on the planet – even those gloomy Eyore types – are quite capable of happiness (as they are of anger, anxiety, fear, boredom, etc). It's just that people experience and express happiness differently.

Happiness is . . .

According to the psychological research, happiness is an emotion. So, before you can actually aspire to achieve this goal, you first need to understand the nature of emotions.

Unfortunately, this isn't as straightforward as it might seem. Although the field of emotions remains one of the biggest research arenas in psychological science, few academics can agree about their nature. In fact, even clarifying the term 'emotion' is so rife with problems that academic psychologists have been prompted to quip that 'everyone knows what an emotion is, until asked to give a definition'.

There are probably a million words and phrases in the English language that colourfully depict our feelings. However, most psychologists agree that we experience no more than a mere handful of separate and distinct emotions.

Emotional breakdown

Most people tend to equate emotions almost exclusively with mood. However, as the CBT paradigm demonstrates, our feelings are also linked to our social and personal situations, our thoughts, our physical sensations, and finally our behaviours. It's unlikely that we're going to experience one without the others being activated in some way.

Let's illustrate this point by looking at a typical CBT emotional reaction. Say you were called upon to give a presentation at work (**social situation**). How would you **feel**? Many people become nervous, sometimes even terrified, when they've been called upon to stand up and address a group.

Now concentrate on what **physical symptoms** are likely to emerge. Sweating palms, perhaps? Breathlessness? Racing heartbeat? Stomach pains? Dizziness? You wouldn't be alone.

Next, focus on what **thoughts** might be running through your mind. Would you be concerned you might fumble with the overhead projector? Look foolish? Forget what you're saying mid-sentence? Humiliate yourself in front of your colleagues and boss? Do you remember back to that time when you froze and couldn't speak at your school debating contest because you were so scared? Again, all typical reactions.

Leading me to my final question: how would you **behave**? Call in sick on the day of the presentation? Beg one of your workmates to take your place? Practise your talk manically? Not surprising. You see, our thoughts, feelings, physiology and behaviours are inextricably linked. So, if we feel a particular way, chances are we're going to think, physically react and behave along similar lines.

You'll have plenty of opportunity to become familiar with the different strands of your emotional responses as this course develops. Right now, though, I just want you to start thinking about the interplay of these different components whenever you experience a feeling.

Why it's good to feel bad sometimes

There's a widespread misconception that only pleasant, positive or happy feelings are healthy, constructive, acceptable and normal. As a result, we've come to think that negative emotions are abnormal, antisocial, and best suppressed and locked away. Nothing could be further from the truth and if you walk away from this program with only one message let it be this. Even though our negative feelings can be painful, extreme and distressing, difficult to cope with sometimes and are often frowned upon by those around us, they are essential to our well-being.

We've been biologically programmed to experience negative emotions and they serve an important purpose. It's just that they get a bad reputation because we're often told as children that being angry or tearful or anxious is socially unacceptable. We're told crying is babyish or unmasculine. That anger is ugly and unfeminine. That sadness is self-indulgent and pathetic. With all this opposition, no wonder we try to hide or suppress our distress.

We're culturally programmed to pretend these things don't exist. But, as we all know, pretending doesn't mean they actually do go away.

Normal though our good and bad emotions might be, you're probably wondering what the point of them is, given their social unacceptability. According to Charles Darwin, our basic emotions, both positive and negative, evolved to promote the survival of the species, because they helped our ancestors respond and react to all kinds of dangerous or threatening situations.

Take fear as an example. Although being terrified is one of the most unsettling and disturbing emotions we can experience, we wouldn't have survived as a species for millions of years without this response.

Here's what I mean. Imagine the scenario. You're walking around an unfamiliar neighbourhood one night to meet some friends for a drink. Although you've been to this wine bar once before, you can't quite remember the exact directions, so you become lost. You end up wandering around lost and alone and, before you know it, you've turned off the main street into a dark lane into a dead-end alley way. Suddenly, you hear footsteps behind you and you turn around to see a large man heading menacingly in your direction. There's no way out.

I'm sure you can imagine the terror you'd be feeling at that moment. Your heart starts to pound so strongly you feel it's going to jump right through your chest. You feel dizzy and breathless, as if you might faint. You begin to shake and break out into a sweat. This is no coincidence because when your mind and body sense danger, they automatically go into red alert. The moment they sense you're under threat, your mind and body let you know in no uncertain terms that you better find an escape route PDQ or be prepared to battle it out. In psychology, we call this the fight or flight response.

This fight or flight response is our innate protection system, which we inherited from our prehistoric ancestors. Back then, of course, they were probably trying to fend off sabre-toothed tigers and other beasts. Nowadays life still has its dangers and threats and we still need a biological warning system. Symptoms of fear or anxiety are often extreme and uncomfortable, but they're designed that way to alert you to sticky situations and save your skin.

How about grief? If you've ever experienced a bereavement, you will know how distressing it is to lose someone close to you. It's normal to feel devastated as you try to adjust to your life without this person. Some people find the pain unbearable and question whether they can go on living themselves. This was the case for one of my clinical clients. This woman, I'll call her Kathleen, had endured a number of serious mental health problems for over twenty years. Anxiety. Depression. Borderline Personality Disorder. Alcohol and drug dependency. She was doing really well for several months, had remained abstinent, settled into a new house, was even thinking about resuming employment. And then one day Kathleen came to an appointment with me and threatened suicide. It turned out her mother had taken her own life just the day before. Since they were very close, Kathleen was understandably shocked and devastated by this sudden development. She missed her mother terribly and couldn't conceive of living in a world without her. So, in Kathleen's mind, the only solution was suicide. The pain would end and she could join her mother in the afterlife.

Luckily, Kathleen and I were able to work through these issues that day and thankfully she's now doing well again. We talked a lot about how grief is the price we pay for loving someone we lose, and that the awful feeling of sadness is a normal reaction to this loss, unbearable and overwhelming and terrifying as it often is.

The anatomy of emotion

When it comes to our feelings, we sometimes talk about our hearts being broken, or of getting that funny sensation in the pit of our stomach, or feeling something ominous in our water, but in fact our brain is the true centre of our emotions. The **limbic system** to be exact.

The limbic system is the bit of the brain which:

1. governs our motivation and memory;

2. serves as a meeting place between our **cortex**, which produces our language, thinking and reasoning abilities, and our **hypothalamus**, which is responsible for our biological drives, such as eating, drinking, body temperature, sexual behaviour and emotional arousal;

3. houses the **amygdala**, which allows us first to evaluate information from the outside world and then determines an appropriate emotional response;

4. includes the **septum**, which helps keep our feelings in check, so they don't go raging out of control, and

5. comprises the **hippocampus**, where memories are formed, allowing us to evaluate a current situation based on past experiences.

Let's look at the limbic system in action by taking the example of meeting potential in-laws for the very first time. A stressful situation if ever there was one.

You're eager to make a good impression on your beloved's ma and pa, so during the drive over your cortex is activated as you anticipate the topics of conversation that will crop up (career, education, your parents) and subject areas that are best avoided (that recent romantic weekend away, your tattoo, and your brief stint as an eco warrior as a student). Your hypothalamus is making you feel a little tense and apprehensive, while your amygdala is busy evaluating those little gems of information you already know about them (rich, conservative and set in their ways). Your septum is helping control your stomach from doing flip-flops and your hippocampus is conjuring up those embarrassing images of the last time you met some people you thought would be your in-laws . . .

Emotional intensity

Have you ever noticed that some people can bounce off the walls with joy, but on other occasions sink into a pit of black misery? And how about those men and women who, whatever the situation, are so laid-back they're practically horizontal?

The degree or intensity of feeling we experience is also part of our emotional make-up. Our emotional patterns are fairly consistent, so if you're the type of person who is euphoric at weddings then I bet you cry buckets during sad movies because we tend to experience positive and negative emotions with equal intensity. If, on the other hand, a joyful occasion brings a quiet smile to your face, then chances are you'll keep your cool when tempers all around you are flaring.

Emotional intensity varies from person to person. You might be the laid-back, even-tempered kind, but your partner might be more passionate, fiery and prone to extremes in the emotional spectrum. Psychologists don't know exactly why people's emotional reactions are so diverse; probably it's a combination of biological factors and personality. And, no doubt, cultural expectations play a huge role in our feelings also. Paul Ekman, an eminent researcher on emotions at the University of California, has conducted countless studies of different groups of people around the world, ranging from North Americans, Europeans, Japanese and even the Fore, a primitive tribe from Papua New Guinea. His studies found that although emotions themselves are universal across the spectrum of human kind, our expression of them is culturally determined and, as a result, varies enormously from country to country.

Funerals, for example, are always upsetting occasions, but they also serve as opportunities to illustrate culturally acceptable displays of emotion. In this case, mourning and grief. In Latin and Mediterranean countries like Italy, Spain and Greece it's perfectly normal, if not mandatory, to wail, faint and express grief as histrionically as possible. To behave otherwise would be tantamount to lack of respect. In sharp contrast, in England, China and Japan such outbursts would be deemed embarrassing and highly frowned upon. Quiet dignity is more the norm.

Here are some other pointers about emotional intensity.

1. There is no right or wrong way to experience emotions. There's only your way.

2. If you accept this you'll have more realistic expectations about your personal capacity for happiness. In other words, you probably won't be brimming over with euphoria and elation if you're fairly even-tempered most of the time. So, an overall sense of contentment is the target you're aiming for here. Likewise, if you're blessed with a fiery, passionate temperament, you can expect to experience intense joy and elation, but you're also likely to feel rage when provoked.

3. Some people perceive their 'highly emotional' reactions as a personality flaw or defect and this makes them feel bad about themselves. Unless your anger turns into aggression or your

sadness is a symptom of clinical depression, then your animated feelings, negative and positive, reflect your emotional intensity. You might have a hair-trigger temper, but I bet your smile lights up the room. So, don't be so hard on yourself.

EXERCISE 4:
EMOTIONAL INTENSITY QUIZ

We've had the theory, now let's look at the practice. How intense are your feelings? To find out, read through the following questions and circle the emotional response that best reflects you.

1. You're expected to preside over a very important busy meeting first thing in the morning at work. All the upper management types are going to be there, so it's an important opportunity for you to shine. However, due to a train cancellation, you're having problems getting to work on time. In fact, there's a real danger that you might miss the meeting entirely. How would you react?

    A.   I'd be so anxious about looking unprofessional and so worried about maybe losing my job, I'd probably hyperventilate with stress.

    B.   I'd be a little concerned, because I hate being late and I know that very senior managers would have travelled long distances just to see me.

    C.   There's not a lot you can do about the trains. I know it's a hassle, but I'm sure they'll understand. They've probably been stuck as well!

2. Your partner has a laissez-faire attitude towards domestic duties. You've been away for a few days on a business trip and when you arrive home it looks like a whirlwind has swept through the place. You, on the other hand, are a real neat freak, and like everything to be in its correct place. How would you react upon seeing the mess?

    A. I'd be absolutely seething. I mean, how difficult is it to clean up after yourself? Wash a few plates? Hang up a coat? Throw newspapers out?

    B. I'd be a bit cool and maybe give him/her the silent treatment for an hour or have a good moan.

    C. I've long ago accepted that my partner is messy so what's the point in getting angry? She's not going to change.

3. You just found out you've been promoted at work. How would you break the news to friends and colleagues?

    A. I'd be so excited, I'd have to rush out and call everyone I know.

    B. I'd be pretty excited, but probably wait until I get home to tell my family and friends.

    C. I'd be pleased, but probably wait for my boss to tell everyone in the office the news.

4. The man or woman of your dreams has finally asked you out. How do you feel?

A.   I'd be so excited, I wouldn't be able to sleep or eat or concentrate on anything else.

B.   I'd be pretty nervous, but look forward to the evening.

C.   I might get a few butterflies on the day of the date, but otherwise I should be pretty calm.

5.   New neighbours have just moved into the flat downstairs. You've invited them over to your place for drinks on several occasions so you can welcome them to the area. However, each time you ask them, they cry off with some excuse. How would you feel?

A.   Really cheesed off. How dare they fob me off when all I've tried to do was be welcoming and neighbourly!

B.   A little on the hurt side. Maybe I'm just being too sensitive, but I have asked them before.

C.   Not too bothered. They probably really are busy and will come knocking when they've got some free time.

This quiz has been designed to give you a brief insight into your particular experience of emotional intensity. So, what pattern emerged? It's pretty obvious, but if you mostly circled As, then you are likely to experience strong emotions. Bs indicate more moderate emotional responses to situations, while Cs are pretty even-keeled no matter what they're up against.

Hanging in the balance

Here's a question for you. What do the playwright George Bernard Shaw and the film star Brad Pitt have in common? Not an obvious pairing at first glance, but both men seemingly came to the same conclusion: that it really is possible to have too much of a good thing. GBS once cracked the remark that a permanent vacation was his idea of torture, while gorgeous, pouting Mr Pitt recently confessed he had crashed and burned following a year of glittering highs, including his wedding to Jennifer Aniston and rave film reviews.

Poor things. Days spent in secluded hideaways. Millions of adoring fans and bulging bank accounts. Fame. Fortune. Public adoration. Somehow, their 'plight' doesn't really tug at the heart-strings, does it?

Well, we shouldn't be too harsh. Before you dismiss this as nothing but the complaining of spoiled primadonnas, you might be surprised to learn there is an underlying truth to their sentiments. Here's why it's possible to have too much of a good thing.

Think about your own life for a moment. Have you ever noticed that following a particularly happy, joyous occasion, say a wedding, the birth of a child or a successful exam result, you feel this exciting, buzzy burst of euphoria but after a few hours or days, the sensation not only wears off, but in some cases is even replaced by the doldrums? Almost as if the pleasant occasion you'd been looking forward to for months was somehow a big let down and anti-climatic in the end? Almost as if the anticipation of the event was more satisfying than the occasion itself?

If so, there's no need to worry. You're not neurotic or excessively negative. Not at all. Biology's to blame. It's physiologically impossible for us to maintain strong degrees of emotion for very long, whether it's anxiety, fear, anger, sadness, surprise, disgust, frustration or even happiness, because our physiology is programmed to strive for an emotional balance or equilibrium. That's why extreme emotions don't last, because our biology is always striving for even kilter. So, while the bad news is we can't sustain high levels of happiness no matter how badly we want to or how hard we try, the good news is we won't stay angry or anxious or down for the long-haul either. In psychology, this process of mood fluctuation to restore emotional equilibrium is referred to as homeostasis.

Our brain has evolved in such a way in order to prevent our emotions from getting out of control. In order to counterbalance the sensation of strong feelings, the body quickly kicks in and produces similar levels of an opposing emotion. So, if you're feeling euphoria, your body will soon begin to dampen down these sensations by producing sadness. If you become really anxious, your body will soon start to kick in with de-stressing agents. You probably won't notice anything drastic happening; instead, you'll just find that your emotions begin gradually to fade. In some cases, however, the opposing emotion will linger. That's why we some-times notice feeling down after a happy occasion. Homeostasis explains these anti-climactic reactions and the doldrums.

Although sex is one of the most pleasurable activities people enjoy, even physical intimacy becomes less pleasurable over time. I'm sure you'll agree that the publications *Penthouse* and the *New Scientist* make odd bedfellows (if you'll forgive the pun). However, a research team keen to study the 'reduced honeymoon effect' placed advertisements in both magazines, asking newly wed couples to record their rate of sexual intercourse during the first year of marriage. The results proved that the excitement of sexual activity between two married people in love diminished very quickly. In the first month, the couples made love on average seventeen times; after a year, however, this figure was reduced to eight. This study gives some credence to the old wives' belief that if couples put a penny into a pot every time they made love during their first year of marriage and took out a penny every time after, the pot would never be empty!

The implications of homeostasis are far-reaching. Advertisers prey upon our inability to remain 'satisfied' for very long and can easily tempt us with bigger, better, newer, nicer products. Homeostasis also explains why we can't sustain the 'buzz' when we engage in other pleasurable activities like shopping, gambling, consuming gourmet food, even vacations and the lifestyles of the rich and famous.

What are the implications of homeostasis for this program? Am I saying it's impossible to achieve lasting happiness? Absolutely not, but understanding the limits of our human capabilities is essential in itself to avoid later frustration and disappointment. Since you've now learned, for example, that negative emotions are essential and normal and that feelings, even strong, frightening ones, are temporary and will fade, you no longer need to feel *unduly* concerned when you're down, fed up or angry, because these sensations will pass. Likewise, you can now accept that euphoric feelings, following even the most joyful of experiences, will eventually fade and may even be temporarily replaced with sadness. This, too, is normal.

You may be wondering, then, what's the point of pursuing this program, since happiness is so fleeting? Don't pack it in just yet. This course isn't about aiming for the buzz. Instead, we want to concentrate on the goal of increasing your overall sense of personal satisfaction, and the assignments in this program are designed with this purpose in mind.

EXERCISE 5:
HOW HAPPY ARE YOU?

One of the reasons why psychology is a credible social and behavioural science rests with the fact that it's evidence-based. This means our theories and methods are based on systematic study, providing proof for our claims. In my profession it's important that we find out the extent to which our patients and clients improve through therapy. So we often use questionnaires, both at the beginning and at the end of our intervention, to measure objectively someone's progress. After all, it would be a huge waste of time, money and expectation if people didn't improve when therapy came to an end. Pre- and post-intervention questionnaires help us ensure this goal.

Now I'm going to ask you to be your own experimental psychologist by completing the following measure. The Happiness Questionnaire, adapted from the original by Michael Eysenck, will not only tell you what your current levels of happiness are, but since I'll ask you to take the test again at the end of the program, it will also allow you to measure exactly how much you've grown and progressed from start to finish.

The Happiness Questionnaire

To take the questionnaire, which will determine your base rate as we say in psychology, find a quiet place, somewhere you won't be disturbed for at least a half an hour. Since you'll be taking the measure again at the end of nine weeks, you might prefer to photocopy the pages or record your answers on a piece of paper or in your journal so you can compare your results.

The questionnaire consists of forty-five statements. Read each item individually and think about how true it is for you. Numbers ranging from 1 to 9 to the right of each statement reflect this degree of accuracy. If the item is completely true for you, then circle the number 9. If it bears no resemblance to your life at all, ring the number 1. If the statement is only somewhat true, then the numbers 2 through 8 indicate various degrees of applicability.

Three more things. First, we're using this instrument solely as a pre-program assessment measure. Although the questionnaire taps into different areas of your life and can highlight those which you'd like to improve, I want you to think of this task only in terms of your base rate scores. Also, be honest with yourself when answering the questions. It's less painful to pretend we're emotionally more content than we sometimes are, but this questionnaire can only help if answered truthfully. Remember, the aim is to help you improve those areas of your life you find wanting, so there'll be plenty of opportunities to make beneficial changes over the next few weeks. Finally, you don't need to deliberate over each question. A few seconds or so should be more than enough. Remember, mark you answers on a scale of 1 to 9; 1 being that you disagree totally with the statement; 9 being that the statement is completely true for you.

1. I am busier than other people. ☐

2. I have numerous leisure activities to occupy me. ☐

3. I am nearly always 'on the go'. ☐

4. I definitely have more friends than most people. ☐

5. I socialise several times in the average week. ☐

6. I really love spending time with other people. ☐

7. I find my work extremely interesting. ☐

8. Time usually flies when I'm working. ☐

9. I usually work very efficiently. ☐

10. My life is carefully organised. ☐

11. I can nearly always lay my hands on important documents. ☐

12. I usually have enough time each week to do what I want to do. ☐

13. I worry more than most people. ☐

14. I usually find it impossible to keep worrying thoughts out of my mind. ☐

15. Life is a very worrying business. ☐

16. I take life very much as it comes. ☐

17. I do not have any great unfulfilled aspirations. ☐

18. I expect the future to be very much like the past. ☐

19. I am generally very optimistic about things. ☐

20. I am confident that my life will turn out well. ☐

21. I generally anticipate that things will turn out for the best. ☐

22. I think about the present much more than I do about the past or the future. ☐

23. The 'here and now' is of absorbing interest. ☐

24. I always try to live 'for the moment'. ☐

25. My friends regard me as well-adjusted. ☐

26. I am nearly always cheerful. ☐

27. I generally 'bounce back' from adversity. ☐

28. I am more outgoing than most people. ☐

29. People think of me as being very sociable. ☐

30. I am a particularly friendly person. ☐

31. I never 'put on an act' with other people. ☐

32. I am content just to be myself. ☐

33. I have no wish to be like anyone else. ☐

34. I do not feel like my problems are insuperable.   ☐

35. I do not waste any of my time envying other people.   ☐

36. I very rarely experience frustration and anger.   ☐

37. I have an intimate relationship.   ☐

38. My family life has been very loving.   ☐

39. I have more exceptionally close friends than most other people.   ☐

40. I always do what I can to be happy.   ☐

41. I regard being happy as the main goal in life.   ☐

42. I would rather live in ignorant bliss than be a miserable genius.   ☐

43. I am much happier than most people.   ☐

44. I am somewhat unhappy much of the time.   ☐

45. I wish I could be happier.   ☐

Finding your happiness score

The scoring for this questionnaire may seem a bit tricky at first, but once you get the hang of it, it's easy.

Statements 1 to 42 are rated in clumps of three, so begin scoring by adding up the scores for items 1, 2 and 3. Write that total down. Next, move on to 4, 5 and 6, add up those scores and write that total down. And so on and so on.

I

nterpreting the scores

Statements 1 to 3 reflect how busy we are. The average score here is 16.5, and if your total is 13 or below, you may want to think about increasing your activity levels because it's been shown that happy people lead active lives.

Statements 4 to 6 look at how much time we spend socialising. Studies have shown that happy people are much more likely to pack their lives with social events. The average score is 17.6. If your total dips below 14, you're probably spending too much time on your own.

Statements 7 to 9 indicate how meaningful and productive our working lives are, both of which are strongly associated with happiness. The average total is 20.9, and if your figures are below 17, then you may want to think about engaging in more activities that give you some sense of purpose.

Statements 10 to 12 look at your abilities to plan and organise. If your combined score is around 16.8, then your skills are considered average in this area. If, on the other hand, your rating total is less than 15, your life might be more chaotic and less structured than you'd like.

Statements 13 to 15 look at your tendency to worry, because fretfulness is linked to unhappiness. There is however, a slight difference in the scoring here, because a lower rating is more likely to reflect personal satisfaction. The average total is 12.6, so if your figure is 16 or over, you probably have difficulties putting troubling thoughts out of your mind.

Statements 16 to 18 focus on your expectations and aspirations, as they are also important factors in happiness. The average rating here is 11.7. However, if your score is below the 8 mark level, you might want to think about goals you'd like to achieve.

Statements 19 to 21 centre on the degree of optimism in your thinking and attitudes. Again, although optimism and happiness are not synonymous, happy people tend to view situations positively. The average score here is 19.8, so if your total is below 17, then you may be excessively pessimistic in your views.

Statements 22 to 24 reflect a tendency to dwell on past mistakes or worry unnecessarily about the future. 14.1 is the average score, but if your rating is 10 or under, then you may have difficulties forgetting about previous difficulties or fretfully anticipating situations that have yet to or might not even occur.

Statements 25 to 27 help determine if you're hardy enough to be able to handle life's adversities. If you score 19.7 or above, you're likely to be someone who can deal with the stresses and strains of modern living. A score of 17 or under, on the other hand, suggests that you might have difficulties coping when under pressure.

Statements 28 to 30 reflect how outgoing and extroverted you are, traits often associated with happiness. The average score is 16.6, but if your rating is under 13 then you are probably shy, withdrawn and introverted most of the time.

Statements 31 to 33 look at your ability to be yourself. 20.5 is the average rating, but if your score is 12 or under, then perhaps you have a tendency to hide behind a social mask or act in a way you think more acceptable to others.

Statements 34 to 36 centre on coping with negative feelings. If your score hovers around the 18 mark, then you are probably the type of person who is able to cope with unpleasant emotions. However, if your rating levels are below 18, then you might well feel overwhelmed by these sensations.

Statements 37 to 39 look at your ability to form close social bonds. If your score is 19.1 or above, then you're probably enmeshed in a few intimate, trusting relationships with others. On the other hand, if you gave yourself a score below 16, then you might have more of a tendency to keep the people in your life at arm's length.

Statements 40 to 42 centre on how much of a priority happiness is for you. If your total here is 19.6 or more, then you've identified being happy as a major life ambition. If, however, you score is less than 16, then you might want to reassess the importance of your personal satisfaction.

Now we turn to **Statements 43 to 45** which look at your overall level of happiness. In order to score these statements, first look at your rating for statement 43 and subtract this number from 10 (for example, if you circled the number 4, then it's 10 minus 4, for your score of 6). Next, take this number and add it to the scores you circled for statements 44 and 45. This then gives you the total figure for this cluster.

Here, the lower the score, the greater your levels of general happiness. If your rating is 12.8 or below, then you're probably pretty satisfied with the way you're life is going. If you've scored 15 or above, however, there's definite margin for improvement.

Remember, though, this score reflects your general level of happiness. So, in other words, even if you feel quite happy with your personal circumstances overall, I bet there are one or two areas of your life you'd still like to improve or develop. Likewise, if you mainly find yourself down in the dumps, you've probably discovered that your situation wasn't quite so bad or bleak as you might have earlier assumed.

PERSONAL TRAITS ASSOCIATED WITH HAPPINESS

An outgoing personality	High level of Education	Employment
An active social life	Hobbies	Positive events

PERSONAL TRAITS ASSOCIATED WITH UNHAPPINESS

Anxious personality	Low status	Being female
Low self-esteem	Poor health	Stressful events

The Building Blocks of CBT – Motivation and Health

Before we begin the tasks and exercises for week two, I'd like you to take a few moments to think about the thoughts and feelings that emerged during the last seven days. What facts did you learn about happiness? What was most helpful? What's been most surprising for you? Were you able to make links between what came up and the situation you currently find yourself in? You don't have to write these answers down or spend too much time pondering about them. Think of it as a brief warm-up exercise before this week's activities.

We're going to explore two main themes this week. When I begin working with a client, I like to assess their motivation levels and belief that change is possible. Our perceptions of ourselves and our abilities are central to the CBT framework, so it's important we check these out. The second part of this week's task will focus on health issues. As you know, our physical well-being is strongly linked to our thoughts, moods, behaviours and personal circumstances, so health is a top priority. More importantly, my clinical experience has demonstrated that there's no point in looking at emotional, social, behavioural or cognitive concerns if my clients aren't first in good physical condition. They simply won't have the energy to concentrate on and carry out the required tasks so it's important that you get plenty of exercise, not only during the course of the program but as a general rule.

Listed below are your tasks for this week, to estimate and enhance motivation and to improve general health and well-being.

1. Self-Esteem Assessment
2. Locus of Control Exercise
3. Benefits of Change Exercise
4. Lifestyle Check-up
5. Physical Exercise
6. Ten to fifteen minutes' relaxation per day
7. Improving Sleep

EXERCISE 6:
ASSESSING YOUR SELF-ESTEEM

First things first: your motivation. The Happiness Questionnaire is a fantastic tool to help open our eyes to areas in our life which may be lacking. It serves as a good indicator of where we'd like to make improvements. Unfortunately, it doesn't tell us how.

So, you might be sitting there thinking that this information is all very well and good for those people with the confidence and courage and energy to go out and make their lives more complete, but what happens if self-esteem is at rock bottom? Well, I don't expect you to snap your fingers and instantly conjure up the drive, dedication and ideal self-image. However, identifying potential areas of personal improvement is only part of the story. Sooner or later, you'll have to go out there and work towards these goals to achieve any sense of real fulfilment. So, if your sense of self-worth is on the shaky side, then the obvious next step is to help you build up some psychological stamina.

Why is self-esteem important? Because our perceptions of

self-worth determine our motivation to achieve our goals. One of the major stumbling blocks preventing people from achieving happiness, whether it's anxiety, fear of looking foolish, lack of motivation or a belief they simply do not deserve happiness, is poor self-esteem and a latent feeling of worthlessness. Since confidence levels can be boosted, and because high self-esteem is inextricably linked to happiness, we can't proceed any further until we examine this issue in more detail.

So, please take the time to complete the following task. Imagine this scenario. You're sailing on a cruise ship around the Caribbean. It's a once-a-lifetime dream vacation and you'll be away at sea for about six months. You'll be docking in exotic ports, wining, dining and dancing with the glitterati, rubbing shoulders with some of the world's most eminent politicians, writers, artists and celebrities. You just know you're going to have the absolute time of your life.

The days and weeks of tropical breezes and glorious sunsets fly by and you've never been more relaxed or happy. One evening, however, the party atmosphere changes dramatically as tragedy suddenly befalls the ship. As you stand there on deck, sipping cocktails with the likes of Queen Elizabeth II, the Pope, Nelson Mandela, Madonna, Stephen Hawking and an unknown yet brilliant young scientist who's just discovered the cure for cancer, the captain frantically emerges with an important announcement.

Disaster has struck. The ship is on the verge of sinking, and, more catastrophically, due to a bumbling catalogue of administrative errors, the captain announces there's only one life jacket on board. Since, as seafaring tradition dictates, the skipper goes down with the ship, the hapless man's got the further unenviable task of deciding which one of the many assembled esteemed and laudable passengers will be saved.

Here's your task: each of the gathered guests, you included, has been given the challenge of justifying to the captain all the reasons why he or she best deserves this one and only life preserver. Each person has been granted only sixty seconds to plead for their life and, even within the limited time allowed, all have given some pretty convincing reasons why they alone should survive and the others perish. The Pope for his global spiritual role. The Queen as both head of the Commonwealth and defender of the Anglican Church. Stephen Hawking for his significant contributions to science. The young scientist with the cure for cancer argues vehemently that his revolutionary treatment will be lost with his death. Suddenly a young couple emerges from below deck. They've just found out that they're going to be parents and had been on the phone to their families so they could share the happy news. They've been trying for years for a baby and beg tearfully that the mother-to-be and her unborn child be spared.

Now it's your turn. You have sixty seconds to demonstrate why your life is the one that should be saved. So, in the space below (or in your notebook), I want you to write all those reasons down. Be as convincing as possible. Your life depends upon it, remember?

1.

2.

3.

4.

5.

6.

7.

8.

9.

10.

Time's up, but don't worry if you didn't come up with ten responses. A few will do. So, were you able to come up with a highly persuasive argument that convinced the captain why you alone deserved to live? Or did you waver? Perhaps you felt that one of the others should be the survivor?

If so, why? Why do these people deserve to live more than you? Take another sixty seconds and write down all the reasons you can think of.

1.

2.

3.

4.

5.

6.

7.

8.

9.

10.

Time's up again. What did you come up with? Want to know the correct answer? The person who deserves the life jacket most is you. Not the man with the cure for cancer. Not the expectant mother. Not Nelson Mandela. Nor the Pope. Not even Madge. None of them.

I'm not saying their lives aren't important, far from it. They're equally important. That's the point. An individual's worth is much more than the sum total of their achievements. Our value as individuals is so much more vast than our perceived positions, roles and accomplishments in life. You may not be a medical marvel or an international freedom fighter or a world-famous entertainer, but one thing's for certain: you have the right to live your life. Maybe you've got dependent children. Maybe you've got a job you love. Maybe your miniature schnauzer is devoted to you. Maybe you bask in the quiet solitude of your garden. Life is life, yours is as valid as the next person's.

Of course, I don't expect you automatically to inject yourself with strong doses of self-esteem simply by completing this exercise. Our sense of self-worth is deeply engrained and usually the product of our childhood, parents, teachers, friends, biology, culture and personality. So, don't expect huge shifts over night. The aim of this exercise, is to be thought-provoking. But as you progress with the program your confidence in yourself and the life you live should soar.

EXERCISE 7:
LOOKING AT YOUR LOCUS OF CONTROL

Linked to high self-esteem and motivation for improvement is our belief that we intrinsically possess the power and the ability to go out and achieve our goals. In psychology, we refer to strong confident attitudes like this as internal locus of control. By contrast, when people feel that they're more strongly dictated to by outside forces, such as fate, employers, partners or parents, and have little ability to determine the course of their lives by themselves, we call this belief system external locus of control.

The internal locus of control is interlinked with high self-esteem and successful goal achievement. How about you? Do you believe that all your personal goals will be achieved with a little bit of effort and some elbow grease? Or do you harbour the persistent attitude that external forces are too overpowering and will only knock you back at every opportunity?

Take a few minutes and jot down on some paper as many of your life's achievements as you can name. Aim for ten. If you can think of more, great, but there's no need to go overboard. If you're struggling and can only name a few, try not to be too harsh on yourself. Remember, most of us aren't Nobel Prize-winning rocket scientists or top captains of industry. It's normal for achievements and successes to be more modest.

1.
2.
3.
4.
5.
6.
7.
8.
9.
10.

If you're like many people, you may have listed exams passed, sporting achievements, getting married, having children, the odd job promotion, maybe even travelling around the world. As long as the event's given you some sense of achievement, fine. Now I want you to think back on all the effort you put in, the hurdles you overcame and the steps required for you successfully to satisfy these ambitions. Congratulate yourself. You've just demonstrated proof of internal locus of control.

Locus of control, like self-esteem, tends to be deeply rooted in our psyches so I don't expect you to shift any negative attitudes you hold about your empowerment overnight. This exercise is primarily to help you begin analysing and sorting through your thoughts and feelings. Sometimes I find my clients can be quite stubborn on this matter. They put their foot down defiantly, refusing to believe they actually possess the ability to improve their lot in life. In fact, when many of my clients begin reflecting on their accomplishments, some still believe they haven't really achieved anything. This isn't because they've plonked themselves down on a couch and spent the past twenty years with a remote control in their hand, flipping through the channels. Far from it. It's usually that they don't recognise or appreciate the value of what they've achieved or are focusing too much on what they haven't achieved.

Or their successes are in the past, so somehow don't count any more. Or it's been too easy for them to realise certain goals.

If you feel that you're devoid of any real achievements, just think of someone who hasn't been able to achieve one of your goals. Even better, someone who's envious of your success. If you've passed your driving test, try having a conversation with someone who's failed it a few times and see if you don't feel a bit of a marvel. Or maybe you'd think nothing of booking a trip to India, Thailand or some other exotic locale, while your best friend is too terrified even to get on an airplane. As for me, I can't cook. Not at all. Can barely boil water without scorching it. Because I'm such a cretin in the kitchen, I'm genuinely impressed, and I mean really amazed, that it's possible for some people to cook a really great meal. What's particularly jarring is when they do it effortlessly!

EXERCISE 8:
BENEFITS OF CHANGE

Our locus of control, like self-esteem, is a pretty persistent belief system which has a powerful influence over the way we conduct our lives. If you have a low opinion of yourself, you're not likely to have much faith in your ability to succeed. Likewise, if you give yourself high ratings in the appraisal, it tends to follow that you'll have pretty strong beliefs about your abilities to achieve your goals. Like our sense of self-worth, our perceptions about our lives are usually instilled in us throughout childhood. Luckily, however, just as it's possible to develop a more positive sense of our own merits, it's equally possible to equip ourselves with the skills to be more proactive about making changes. Throughout this program, I'll be showing you all the necessary steps to take more control over your life and develop new skills, leading to more positive self-worth.

For now, I want you to ignore your self-perceptions and locus of control constraints and concentrate instead on your degree of motivation. By this, I mean I want you to think about all the benefits of change and the improvements to your life you'd like to see, whether or not you deep down believe they'd ever happen. This can be magic wand time. So ask yourself, how much do you want to be happy? More in control of your life? To achieve the goals you've always dreamed of? The point of this exercise is to begin to allow yourself to question long-held beliefs and have the freedom to consider new and positive alternatives. In time, this will seem more and more attainable.

These questions aren't merely about self-worth or views on capability, they reflect a desire to change. In my clinical practice, I work with clients with persistent and severe mental and physical health problems. Many of my patients also have substance misuse problems – alcohol, heroin, crack, tranquillisers – and my starting point with each of them is assessing their motivation by looking at their views on how much better their lives would be if improvements were made. I can't stress this point enough. Without motivation, maximum benefit is all but non-existent. And motivation has to come from you. All I provide is the information and advice to guide you on your way. The dedication and commitment are yours.

So, take a few minutes and write down in your notebook the answers to the following questions:

What are all the benefits of participating in this program to myself?

How would my family, my friends and my work colleagues also benefit?

How would my physical health, my self-esteem and other areas of my life improve?

What's the biggest benefit for me?

What concerns do I have?

How would I be able to overcome these obstacles?

Motivation, crucial though it is for inspiring us to make major improvements in our life, is a funny kind of thing. Whether it's a diet, giving up smoking, embarking on a physical fitness regime or reining in our finances, we often start off highly enthusiastic about our lifestyle changes but sooner or later motivation levels start to wane. So on Monday morning we're dead keen, focused and resolutely, if not virtuously, determined to become slim, nicotine-free, go to the gym and balance our cheque book. But by Monday lunchtime it's, well, usually a different kind of story. Those profiteroles are simply too irresistible. We convince ourselves that one cigarette won't hurt. The gym and the budgeting? Well, there's always tomorrow, isn't there?

Even with the best intentions and the highest degree of determination, motivation levels fluctuate and sooner or later can peter out. While a lot of people blame themselves for what they see as their lack of discipline, lapses of motivation usually have nothing to do with character weakness. Remember earlier I talked about homeostasis? The same principle applies here. Besides, it's not always easy to stay focused in the beginning when we make lifestyle changes because it often takes a little while to see tangible benefits or improvements. In other words, we feel the pain without seeing any of the gain. It doesn't happen instantly so, to keep yourself focused and motivated during this program, I want you to keep this list of all the benefits you hope to reap. Read it through every week to remind yourself and keep your interest levels raised.

Exercise 9:
Lifestyle check-up

With your motivation levels checked, it's now time to persevere with this week's second theme: health.

CBT is the ultimate strong body/strong mind program, so let's take a closer look at your physical state.

1. Do you smoke?
2. Do you drink excessively? (over 14 units per week if you're female; 21 units if you're male)?
3. Are you taking any prescription drugs?
4. Are you relying on illegal substances?
5. How many cups of coffee do you drink in a day?
6. How are your levels of stress?
7. Do you eat a healthy diet?
8. Do you exercise regularly?
9. Are you getting a good night's sleep?

Here's to good health

If this brief checklist has prompted any concerns about your health, I would recommend making an appointment with your doctor straight away. On a more general level, let's consider some possible lifestyle changes that would contribute to greater physical well-being.

Smoking

Are you still smoking? Surely, surely, no one has to warn you again about the dangers of cigarettes? Although Oscar Wilde once hailed this habit as the perfect pleasure, it quickly loses its sybaritic appeal when you think about lung cancer, emphysema, throat cancer and all the other serious illnesses that cigarettes cause. Not to mention the brown teeth, the bad breath, stinking clothes and nicotine-stained fingers.

Why persist with a nasty, harmful habit? Although smokers often swear blind that cigarettes calm them down, help them concentrate and make them feel better, this is really just their addiction talking. The irritability, difficulties focusing the mind and jitteriness commonly experienced between cigarettes are symptoms of nicotine withdrawal, which quickly disappear within seconds of lighting up.

Even if you've tried quitting and failed in the past, keep trying. Studies have shown it often takes a number of attempts before kicking the habit is successful. Consider nicotine replacement therapy, Stop Smoking programs, hypnotherapy. Seek advice from your doctor.

Alcohol

While the positive health benefits of moderate drinking have been well-documented, particularly red wine in the cases of middle-aged men and post-menopausal women, over-indulging clearly has its dangers. Not only does excess alcohol intake impair the liver, cause certain types of cancer and decrease brain function, mood is also affected. Alcohol is a depressant, after all, and many symptoms of low moods and depression clear up quickly following abstinence from the demon drink. Excessive drinking also interferes with sexual function.

Drugs

Prescription medications and illegal drugs (marijuana, cocaine, heroin, ecstasy among others) can also impair your health. All drugs, even the prescription kind, have side effects and toxic properties that can take their toll on your physical and mental well-being, especially if you've been taking them for a while. Even those, like tranquillisers, which are prescribed to lift mood can lead to addiction and, paradoxically, an increase in anxiety.

If you find your health spiralling downwards, drugs might be to blame. Should you notice any worrying symptoms which you feel might be linked to prescription or recreational drugs, always discuss your concerns with your doctor. He or she could probably prescribe another medication with fewer side effects or discuss alternative treatment options. If addiction is a worry, they would give you informative advice on detox and rehab options.

Caffeine

Many people can't bear thinking about starting their day without a cup or two (or three or four) of coffee. Because it's so commonplace and widely available in our society, we sometimes forget that caffeine is a powerful, mildly addictive substance that can pose problems for our body and mind. Although some people swear they need this stimulant to kick start them in the morning and make them feel normal, others complain it dampens their mood. I would recommend either eliminating caffeine from your daily intake entirely or, if you simply can't face that prospect, reduce your consumption to one or two cups a day. To avoid withdrawal symptoms like jitteriness, irritability and fatigue, cutting down your intake gradually, say by one cup a day, will be less drastic for your system.

Identifying and coping with stress

Stress seems to be the scourge of the modern age. We can hardly pick up a book or magazine without some reference to the extreme demands and pressures we face daily.

Although a certain amount of stress is not only beneficial but vital to our lives – otherwise we'd never be motivated to get out of bed in the morning – when we're overwhelmed and having difficulties coping, our health is in danger. Asthma, ulcers, diabetes, depression, nausea, arthritis, influenza and colds, hypertension, heart disease, stroke and cancer have all been linked to stress. In fact, studies have even shown that stress makes our brains shrink!

The first step to combating stress is to identify the sources of pressure in your life. Have a look at the following list of stressors. According to researchers Holmes and Rahe, these are the top twenty life events which are most likely to impact on our well-being.

1. Death of a spouse
2. Divorce
3. Marital separation
4. Prison term
5. Death in the family
6. Marriage
7. Job loss
8. Retirement
9. Marital reunion
10. Family illness
11. Pregnancy
12. Sexual problems
13. New family member
14. Business problems
15. Change in economic situation
16. Death of a friend
17. New job
18. Increased marital conflict
19. Mortgage
20. Mortgage foreclosure

The first step in overcoming stress is to identify the reasons you're feeling overwhelmed in the first place. We often place upon ourselves hugely unrealistic demands and expectations in terms of our time, energy and commitments. Learning to manage stress means learning how to prioritise. If you only accomplish three or four tasks in a day, make sure they're the most important. The others can be relegated to another time.

Try to look at the bigger picture. Some of our stressors are long-term. On our list, death of a loved one, marital breakdown, family illness, prison, retirement and business difficulties usually fit into this category. Other stress factors are more short-term. New job, meeting a new family member and mortgage foreclosure fit this bill along with job interviews, blind dates, starting at a new school and public speaking. The long-term stressors are much more likely to be harmful and hazardous to your health and many people undergoing such pressures turn to destructive coping mechanisms – excessive alcohol, drugs, smoking, comfort eating – which in turn only fuel the negative situation. If this is the case for you, you might like to speak to a counsellor or psychologist who can help you with stress management programs so you'll learn to handle the pressures more effectively.

Getting in on the action

Exercise is not only a great stress buster and fitness enhancer, it also promotes emotional well-being. When we exercise, our body produces chemicals called endorphins. Often referred to as 'nature's pain killers' or even 'the runner's high', endorphins are released after about twenty minutes of exercise. I therefore strongly advise you to take up thirty minutes of exercise every day – that's if your doctor gives you the go-ahead.

If this recommendation seems too drastic for your current lifestyle or you've been sedentary for quite a while, don't worry. Even a brisk walk will make a difference to your physical and emotional well-being. If this still seems like too much of an endurance test, then try starting off with an exercise regime of twenty minutes three times a week. You'll notice real benefits in a few weeks, I promise.

One of my former clients, a tough customer if ever there was one, balked at this advice: 'I never feel better after I've done physical exercise, doctor. I always feel worse. The aches, the pains, the fatigue . . . who needs it? Now, drinking, smoking and eating some delicious food, that's when I feel better!'

A common sentiment, I can assure you, but after three weeks of bellyaching even he became a convert. That's because the gain very quickly catches up with and surpasses the pain. The more you commit yourself to the regime, the stronger, more alert and happier you'll feel. There are so many forms of exercise to choose from, I'm sure you'll be able to find one you can tolerate and even enjoy given half a chance.

The following list should help you choose:

Swimming
Aerobics
Dancing
Football
Walking
Martial arts
Tennis
Racquetball
Jogging
Weight training
Yoga
Rowing
Biking
Skating
Netball
Volleyball

You could also try visiting your local sports centre for suggestions. Of course, if you have any pre-existing conditions, such as heart problems or asthma, or if the exercise bike and weights have been collecting dust in the corner for a long time, then seek your doctor's advice before you start. He or she might even recommend specific exercise programs that would be suitable for your age and level of fitness.

Relaxation

We're all so busy rushing and racing around there never seems to be enough time to get everything done, or even think about taking a break, collecting our thoughts or just unwinding.

Try as we might, we can't accomplish everything, but it doesn't stop us from piling on the pressure. One way of coping with these incessant demands is through relaxation, which is the cornerstone of most stress management programs. Studies have shown that people who regularly take part in relaxation exercises report significant improvements in their concentration levels, reduction in stress and peace of mind.

So, your next task, in addition to your daily exercise program, is to set aside ten to fifteen minutes every day for relaxation. Even if your life is jam-packed with job, kids, dog, domestic duties, you should still find at least ten minutes to unwind and clear your mind. Some of my clients like to start the day, either when they first get up in the morning or when they first go into their office, with a few minutes of quiet time just to collect their thoughts. Others like to take their relaxation break during their lunch hour when they can go to a nearby park and get some fresh air. Some prefer to unwind in this way before they go to bed. It doesn't matter. Everybody's schedule is different so fit this time in when you can.

For maximum benefit, I would recommend buying a relaxation tape, especially one with guided visualisation techniques, but some people feel just sitting quietly and undisturbed is sufficient. Whatever you choose, keep in mind that sometimes our thoughts wander. All kinds of things might pop into your head. Your business meeting tomorrow. Picking up the kids from swimming lessons. Walking the dog. Cooking supper. Whatever. When you find your mind straying, just gently refocus your attention back to the tape's message.

Sleeping easy

There's nothing like a good night's sleep to make us feel better. However, it often surprises people when they learn that scientists have yet to discover the precise reasons why we need sleep at all. Some suggest it's a throwback to our prehistoric days to prevent us from stumbling around in the dark and getting eaten by dinosaurs. Others argue sleep facilitates dreaming, which in turn helps us sort through the thoughts, worries and concerns that have been brought up during the day. Sleep also helps repair the wear and tear on our bodies.

We may not fully understand the exact purpose of sleep, but without it we're likely to feel irritable, bad-tempered, distracted, fatigued and lacking in co-ordination. Sleep deprivation can even lead to hallucinations.

Your next challenge, therefore, is to improve the quality of your sleep. Although sleep is one of our strongest biological drives, insomnia seems to be on the increase. Many people, particularly those who are anxious, worried, depressed or stressed, reveal they spend more time watching the clock till the small hours then getting some shut eye, so here are some tips.

1. Recent studies have shown that around 66 percent of the population is not getting enough sleep. Although the required amount varies between people – Margaret Thatcher, for

instance, was notoriously able to get by on just four or five hours a night – eight to ten hours is considered the normal, healthy range.

2. Try restricting your coffee consumption to the mornings or at latest early-afternoons. The effects of caffeine, whether from coffee, tea or chocolate, can last for several hours. That 4 p.m. pick-me-up can prevent you from drifting off to sleep at 11.

3. If you can't fall asleep, get up and go to another room. Try listening to the radio, watching television or reading a good book. Activities like these are great for calming the mind, especially since insomnia can make people stressed, which in turn will keep them awake. However, it's important that you get up and leave your bedroom and only return when you're drowsy. Because we rely on environmental cues to help us drift off to sleep – think about those restless nights when staying with friends in an unfamiliar room or in a strange hotel during a business trip – you want your bedroom to be associated with sleep, not sleeplessness.

4. Alcohol can also disturb your sleep patterns, making them more shallow which in turn prevents adequate rest. So, another good reason not to uncork another bottle of that tantalising red.

5. Avoid heavy dinners and desserts because they will send wakeful signals to the brain.

6. Try not to engage in heated or lively discussions or watch a tense thriller right before you go to bed. Instead, focus on activities that will help ease the mind, maybe reading a book or listening to the radio.

7. Check that the temperature in the room is comfortable. Being too hot or too cold can interrupt sleep.

8. Don't rely on sleeping pills. They don't provide restorative, beneficial sleep. Instead, they drug you to knock you out. Besides the next morning you'll wake up with a drowsy, hungover feeling.

9. Although many people believe hot baths are the perfect antidote for insomnia, they should actually be avoided right before bedtime. The heat from the water will dilate the blood vessels and invigorate the body.

HAPPINESS MYTH NO. 1: PEOPLE WHO ARE SERIOUSLY ILL OR WHO HAVE PHYSICAL DISABILITIES ARE MORE MISERABLE

While a serious disability or physical illness has an enormous and devastating impact on someone's life, adversely affecting day-to-day routine, such people are not necessarily more prone to unhappiness. Any negative emotional fallout is likely to occur within the first few weeks or months of the disability or illness, but following a period of adjustment, normal mood levels tend to return. Remember homeostasis? And remember that negative emotional reactions are normal in times of adversity?

This applies even in the case of chronic disease. Michael J. Fox, one of America's best-loved entertainers, has bravely spoken out about his struggle with Parkinson's Disease. A debilitating and distressing illness, Parkinson's affects our central nervous system.

The cardinal symptoms are usually tremors and shakiness, muscle rigidity, difficulties in moving and flatness of facial expression. Although most often associated with the elderly, Michael J. Fox is proof positive that the disease can strike anyone irrespective of age, wealth or social status.

In his recent autobiography, he voices his original fears, anxieties and distress when forced to come to terms with the diagnosis. He records heavy drinking and shutting out even those closest to him, revealing his initial fears that his wife would abandon him in his hour of need. All very understandable and normal reactions to this frightening diagnosis.

However, in choosing to address his fears and not suppress them, Fox has bravely picked up the pieces of his life and now works tirelessly as a spokesman, advocating an increase in research funding and enhancing public awareness of the illness. He has also achieved a greater appreciation of the positive forces in his life: his wife and children. Parkinson's may have a great and profound impact on his life and I'm sure every day poses new struggles. But the disease doesn't define him as a human being nor does it constitute his whole life.

Week Three:
The Building Blocks of Happiness

Welcome to week three. Before we launch into our latest themes and goals, I want you to take a few moments first to think about your progress so far. How are you feeling? Chances are you might not be at your absolute physical best just now. Your muscles are probably aching from introducing exercise into an otherwise sedentary lifestyle. You might feel shaky and irritable if you're trying to give up nicotine and alcohol and other substances. You probably feel tired and headachey if you've cut down or cut out caffeine. Don't worry. As your body becomes better adjusted to healthier ways, it's normal to feel like this.

The good news is that the aches and pains are temporary and they're actually a sign that your body is healing and becoming stronger. Besides, you're probably finding that daily relaxation and improved sleep are providing some welcome relief and restoration. I'd therefore like you to carry on with:

1. Looking after your physical health
2. Thirty minutes of physical exercise at least three times per week
3. Ten to fifteen minutes' relaxation everyday
4. Improving sleep

I've subtitled this week's activities 'the building blocks of happiness', and all the tasks and exercises here are designed to help you increase your capacity for personal satisfaction.

EXERCISE 10:
THE MIRROR EXERCISE

Facial Feedback Theory

Day 1 and 2

Your first task of the week is called the mirror exercise. Since the goal of this program is for you to *be* happy, not just appear happy, your first exercise of the week is one that will help you develop genuine feelings of happiness. I'm not talking about the buzzy thrill of instant gratification. Our target here is a sense of emotional balance.

The mirror exercise is simple and, because it works on your physiology, highly effective.

On days 1 and 2, I want you to stand in front of a mirror and simply look into your eyes for two minutes. Yup. That's it. Stare at yourself for two whole minutes. What could be easier?

As you stand there, however, you might find that your thoughts begin to wander. You might start to think about the latest news reports or that steak you'll need to defrost for dinner or your dental appointment later that morning. That's okay, but as soon as your thoughts start to stray, gently redirect your thoughts and focus once again on looking into your eyes.

Since most people aren't narcissists you may initially feel a little silly or self-conscious gazing at yourself in this way, but don't be put off. This exercise is enormously beneficial. No, I'm not trying to promote vanity, but it may surprise you to know that 90 percent of all communication is non-verbal. And, what's more, the majority of these messages, whether thoughts, feelings or intentions, are expressed through our facial features, especially our eyes. When people are unhappy, particularly if they've been downcast for a while, their negative mood shines through even before they've uttered a single word. So the main aim of this particular segment of the task is to help you gain some insight into your own non-verbal cues.

Days 3 and 4

I once read something interesting, if not telling, about the salient differences between males and females. When men look at their faces in the mirror, they only register their attractive features. Women, on the other hand, only notice their flaws!

This little observation is relevant because on days three and four, I want you to gaze at your entire face. Still looking in the mirror. Still for the full two minutes. So, men, try not to get too carried away blowing kisses at your perfect visage – tempting though it is, I'm sure – and, women, try not to become too bogged down by that new pimple or the way your nose veers off to the left. Chances are, they're not as bad as you're making them out to be anyway. Once again, however, if your mind starts to wander in this way, gently direct your thoughts back to studying your face.

Days 5, 6 and 7

Another slight change. From day 5 onwards, I now want you to smile at yourself in the mirror for the full two minutes. That's right, smile. And I mean a genuine and warm smile. I know a true, heartfelt grin might be a bit difficult to muster in the beginning, you might feel silly, but this exercise won't work if all you can manage is a forced, false kind of social smile. If you feel self-conscious about spontaneously flashing your teeth, you might find it easier to start off with a small grin.

The physiological and emotional benefits of smiling

Since it's not my normal practice to encourage people to engage in inane antics for no good reason, I assure you there are plenty of important reasons why I've asked you to do the mirror exercise. In fact, the mere act of smiling produces physiological changes that enhance happiness.

1. Smiling enhances our facial features. When people have been unhappy for quite a while or haven't had much to smile about, their faces become set, they can look quite stern – even if they don't mean to – and their muscles atrophy. The mirror exercise will help you build up and strengthen the muscles in your cheeks, making smiling easier and more natural.

2. With practice, smiling will become more spontaneous, reflexive and automatic – your default facial feature. Many of my clients, particularly those who describe themselves as chronically unhappy, rarely smile. As a result, they come across as miserable and unapproachable. In other words, the very people others go to great lengths to avoid. Frequent smiling and a cheerful tone of voice are not only the non-verbal cues most often associated with happiness, they are also more likely to draw people to you.

3. The mere act of smiling is itself a mood enhancer. Benjamin Franklin once observed that 'a cheerful face is nearly as good for an invalid as healthy weather', and this is no mere old wives' tale. According to the facial feedback theory, our facial expressions have an impact on our emotional well-being. Not

only are our facial features linked to a particular emotion – such as smiling when we're happy or frowning when we're sad – but they may even induce the mood. Because our emotions produce corresponding degrees of muscle tension in our facial expressions – more relaxed when we're happy, tenser when we're stressed – the brain uses this sensory feedback system to produce the appropriate feeling. In other words, it's not the mind that determines how we feel, but rather out expressions telling the brain.

In a study conducted by two researchers, McCann and Anderson, in support of the facial feedback theory a group of participants was asked to visualise a series of both happy and unhappy scenarios. The pleasant ones included imagining top academic grades, winning the Lottery and meeting their dream partner, and the unpleasant ones comprised the death of a parent, the loss of a close friendship and the amputation of a limb.

The individuals were asked both to smile and to restrict smiling when they thought of the happy scenarios, and to frown and refrain from frowning when they visualised the unhappy scenes. When asked to report how they felt, the subjects revealed they felt less enjoyment when thinking about the pleasant scenarios on those occasions they restricted themselves from smiling than when they were allowed to smile. Likewise, they felt more distress when permitted to frown during the unpleasant scenarios and less unhappiness when they suppressed the frowning.

Check it out for yourself. Smile for a few moments. Then try frowning. Notice the difference in muscle tension? How does this tension affect your mood?

EXERCISE 11:
RANDOM ACTS OF SMILING

One of the major strengths of CBT is its emphasis on teaching people how to be their own therapists and problem solvers. CBTers don't just talk about it, they go out and do something about it. So, since actions often speak louder than words, now you've practised the smiling in the mirror exercise, I want you to go public.

Have you ever noticed how unhappy and grim the general public often seems? Whether on the train, in the bank or walking down the street, the looks on people's faces often just scream out misery. A few years ago, I came up with a hypothesis. What if people weren't really as miserable or irritable as they seemed? Instead, I wondered if they were just too self-conscious or fearful of possible rejection from others should they smile first. I realise unexpected overtures of cheer and goodwill are risky and can be met with suspicion. However, I queried, could this perpetuation of misery be halted? What would happen if some brave soul dared to be the first one to smile?

So, in the name of psychological science, I set myself to conduct a social experiment – my random acts of smiling experiment – to find out how people would react if I smiled and was pleasant to them. Over the course of a few weeks, every time I bought a newspaper, purchased a train ticket, went shopping, ordered food in a restaurant, whatever, I purposely went out of my way to be cheerful and friendly. And the results were pretty amazing. Ninety percent of people I encountered responded in kind. In fact, even the downright grumpy types usually came around pretty quickly as I persisted in smiling and being friendly even when they snapped and snarled. And you know what else? The newsagent would reserve the last copy of my daily newspaper for me. Tables in overbooked restaurants would suddenly materialise out of thin air. I'd get extra treatments free from the hairdresser. Smiling works in all kinds of beneficial ways.

Smiling also affected my own behaviour. Not only would people respond more positively when they were first greeted in a friendly, cordial way, but after a succession of pleasant encounters I myself also felt much more inclined and willing to carry on engaging in this cheery behaviour. This is no accident. In addition to the facial feedback effect of smiling, another psychological process was occurring: reinforcement. In other words, the psychological process in which other people's reactions to our behaviours have an impact on the way we behave in the future. Since people smiled back at me (positive reinforcement), I was encouraged to carry on with my random acts of smiling. And still do so.

On day 6 of this week, you should go out and do the same thing. Don't worry. I'm not going to ask you to approach total strangers. Instead, every time you have a typical conversational exchange with a shopkeeper or receptionist or bank clerk or café waiter, try being cheerful. There's no need to be excessively jolly or come across as manically hyper-friendly. You don't have to worry about making conversation, just a pleasant 'good morning' or 'hello' is all that's required. Even if you're met with a grumpy response, persist.

EXERCISE 12:
EXCHANGING GOOD NEWS

How did you get on with the smiling exercise? I'll bet you found that most people greeted you with a genuine grin in return. But smiling is merely one tool in the happiness toolbox.

Here's another exercise linked to the facial feedback theory and the positive reinforcement of happiness. Starting on day 7, all you need to do is exchange a piece of good news with a friend or relative every day. The actual topic itself doesn't really matter, and there's no need to launch into a major league sermon endlessly extolling the beauties of the universe or the boundless joys of stamp-collecting. If you're strapped for topics, you might just want to comment on a nice evening out with a friend or an enjoyable film you went to see. As long as it's a daily dose of good news.

Why is this important? Because this exercise will force you consciously to focus on some pleasant events going on in your life or happening somewhere in the world. It is a good foundation for building positive thoughts which, in turn, impact on your mood.

In CBT terms, as you know by now, our perceptions and attitudes are central to our feelings about ourselves, other people and the world around us. Although we will be looking at these processes in much greater detail throughout this book, it's helpful to keep reminding ourselves that our moods have an impact on the way we think. And if we're feeling gloomy and pessimistic then our thoughts are going to be correspondingly negative and self-defeating. What's more, when we're feeling down and thinking pessimistic thoughts, we also tend to magnify the bad in the world and minimise the good. In psychology, we call this catastrophising.

There's another reason why exchanging good news with each other boosts our spirits. Professor Paul Gilbert from the University of Derby, an expert in the field of mood disorders, has found that the mere fact of interacting with others has beneficial properties when it comes to our own happiness. So, we mix with others, we feel better. We mix with others and exchange good news, we feel great.

EXERCISE 13:
REVISITING YOUR OBSTACLES TO HAPPINESS

This is the final exercise of the week. Take about fifteen minutes and once again consider your beliefs about being happy. Look back at your notes for Exercise 8. Do any lingering doubts about your pursuit of happiness emerge? Are they still as strong as they were before you began this course? Are they less so? How might you overcome these blocks?

HAPPINESS MYTH NO. 2:
YOUNG PEOPLE ARE HAPPIER THAN OLDER ADULTS

Although it is widely held that young people are the envy of the middle-aged and the elderly because they have youth on their side, live carefree lifestyles and seem to have endless fun, freedom, romance and time, the truth is exactly the opposite. Actually, contentment and personal satisfaction increase with age. So, here's to growing old gracefully, disgracefully, or any way we can.

Promoting Positive Change

Welcome to week four. Before we carry on with this week's themes and goals, I want you to take a few moments to consider the tasks of the past few weeks. How are you getting on with the exercises, particularly the social experiments? How did people respond when you approached them with a cheerful hello? And what about the exchange of good news? How have these experiences influenced your own attitudes and behaviours? It's still early days, but I would wager you're starting to feel better already.

This week, I'd like you to carry on with some of the other activities introduced in the previous three weeks. Like acquiring any new skill, you'll have to work to achieve true happiness so it's important that you incorporate the following tasks into your weekly schedule for maximum benefit:

1. Looking after your physical health
2. Thirty minutes of physical exercise at least three times per week
3. Ten to fifteen minutes' relaxation every day
4. Improving sleep
5. Mirror exercise
6. Random acts of smiling
7. Exchanging good news

The theme of week four is promoting positive change. We do this in two ways. First, one of the main aims of CBT is to push boundaries and encourage us to venture out of the safe confines of our comfort zones. Even though we might be unhappy with our present circumstances, there's still something familiar, predictable, and therefore appealingly safe about staying put. It's not that we're happy in our misery, more that we're inured to our own discomfort. It's this self-imposed prison I want to free you from. The second main theme this week, which reinforces the first target, is to help you construct healthier, more positive and beneficial belief structures about your right to happiness and the possibilities of change.

Exercise 14:
Seek a new interest

Ready to break free from your comfort zone? Because the first task this week is to take up a hobby or interest. They provide all kinds of benefits. Not only do interests and activities spark up our life and increase our confidence, the psychological research consistently shows that happy people almost universally have outside interests.

Even if it's just once a week for an hour, not only will you spend your time doing something you enjoy, which in itself does wonders for your mood, but hobbies have a way of holding our attention to such an extent that we feel calm and relaxed. In other words, the mere act of focusing your mind on and actively engaging in some pleasurable activity will contribute to your overall sense of happiness. A noted psychologist with the remarkably unpronounceable name Csikszentmihalyi, referred to this total sensory immersion process as 'flow experience'. In other words, we're so engrossed with what we're doing, time flies and we pretty much forget everything else around us.

Maybe you've been thinking for a while about rekindling an interest in something you once upon a time enjoyed, like painting watercolours or playing a musical instrument, or perhaps you've been putting off signing up for that Thai cooking class at your local community centre. Now's your chance.

Many people, especially those who have low moods, often have difficulty even naming a hobby. They tell me they're not interested in anything. If this resonates with you, it is probably more symptomatic of feeling unhappy (for all the reasons I noted earlier about the negative mood/negative thinking link) than of actual fact. But if you're really having a tough time coming up with a potential hobby, you could try one of two options. First, you could hark back to the past and think about the hobbies you used to enjoy as our interests tend to be enduring. If that option brings you no joy, try phoning up your local community college or adult education centre. They usually have dozens of classes on the go, ranging from Aromatherapy to Zen Buddhism. You're bound to find something.

Just remember, any hobby or interest, at least once every week.

EXERCISE 15:
REVISITING YOUR PERCEPTIONS
AND BELIEFS ABOUT HAPPINESS

As you get into the groove of your newfound hobby, I want to devote the remainder of the week to working on your belief systems to promote health and happiness.

Earlier, I asked you to spend some time thinking about the obstacles to your happiness and no doubt you've been able to identify at least one or two beliefs that truly hold you back and keep you confined in your comfort zone. Or maybe you can't quite yet articulate what your attitudes are, but you've got this funny, unsettling feeling somewhere in the pit of your stomach that keeps you from moving forward.

Don't worry if that's the case. Our beliefs about ourselves, the world and other people are so deeply embedded in our psyches that we're not always consciously aware of them. With a bit of practice and concentration, however, they will eventually emerge and enter into our conscious arena. The following exercise will help you identify them.

The birth of our beliefs

Our beliefs tend to be engrained and elusive for the simple reason that they're usually formed during childhood and over many years incorporated into our cognitive and emotional landscape, so much so we accept them without question.

Why do some people harbour negative views about striving for happiness? Maybe, while growing up, you were harshly told off whenever you asked for something you wanted, or maybe led to believe that your personal happiness wasn't important and branded selfish even for having these expectations. Or perhaps parents and teachers tried to protect you from potential disappointment by advising you not to set much store on what you saw as happiness. Maybe they themselves had experienced disappointment or failure in the past and were trying their best to ensure you didn't suffer similar setbacks.

Perhaps, as a result, there's a little voice inside your head today that whispers in admonishment 'this won't last', 'you have no right to be happy', or 'you'll have no one else to blame but yourself when all this goes wrong', every time you even dare to experience a pang of longing for happiness.

The power of these beliefs is so deep they become automatic to us, a constant reminder of all the reasons we can't have happiness, forever pointing to the evidence of past disappointments and failures. Maybe, for example, that dream job you pinned all your hopes on turned out instead to be a nightmare. Perhaps Mr Right turned out to be Mr Disastrously Wrong. Life is full of such experiences and we learn valuable lessons from them. But that relentless little critical voice pipes up with an 'I told you so!' just when we need it least. Not only does it kick us when we're down, it seems to confirm our worst fears.

There is good news, I promise. Negative beliefs and unhealthy attitudes can actually be changed and replaced with constructive, enabling ones. Beliefs that actually work in our favour. Just because we have these self-defeating cognitions lurking in the back of our minds somewhere, this doesn't mean they're true. Nor are we stuck with them for good.

Changing negative beliefs

Step One: Accessing the subconscious

Here's how we take the first steps towards initiating change: we make our deeply entrenched self-limiting attitudes available to our conscious mind. This means rooting around inside our sub-conscious for a bit, so we can identify what they are.

Brainstorming is very useful here, so now I'd like you to go and get hold of a very large piece of paper. At the top, in big letters, write 'My attitudes towards happiness'.

Next, set your watch, alarm clock or an egg timer for ten minutes. In this time, I want you to write down all your beliefs, perceptions, feelings and thoughts about happiness. The good. The bad. The silly. The absurd. The reasonable. I don't care what they are or where you get them from. Songs, movies, books, your neighbour, your parents, plays, art, any source of inspiration will do. At this point we're only after quantity, not quality, so if it pops into your head, write it down.

Try to avoid itemising all your beliefs in a neat list. Aim for the creative and the disorganised instead. Since we're accessing the subconscious mind, we don't have to be analytical or logical. In fact, it's counterproductive to be so. Instead, try using multi-coloured pens, altering the size and shape of letters, write at different angles, spread your answers all across the page. You could even try writing with the other hand, because even this action will access different parts of the brain.

Remember to take the full ten minutes. Sometimes, our most meaningful, poignant thoughts and feelings don't burst forth until the final moments.

Working with the subconscious can be tricky; we have to approach it differently. So, if you're having trouble getting the hang of it, here are two tips. You could try referring back to the first week's section on happiness beliefs. Alternatively, you might want to try putting this exercise aside for a while and focus your thoughts on something else. Going for a walk. Cooking some lunch. Reading a book. Taking a bath. These activities will help unblock your mind and you'll probably find the answers pop into your head before long. This happens all the time. In psychology, we call this process the Eureka! or Aha! effect, because our solutions seem to hit us from out of the blue.

Step Two: Reviewing your beliefs

I now want you to scan through your beliefs and cross out all those that don't really strike a strong chord with you.

Next I'd like you to group all your positive and negative beliefs separately. Listing them one after the other will probably make it easier to concentrate. So, in your positive cluster, you might have written attitudes like:

'Happiness makes life worthwhile.'

'Being happy would improve the rest of my life.'
'Happiness is the highest goal to aim for.'
'Being happy should help make it easier to cope.'
'Being happy will benefit the other people in my life.'
'Happiness is something I'm capable of and deserve.'

And some of your negative beliefs might resemble these:

'Looking for happiness is pointless.'
'You're either born happy or you're not. You can't choose
    happiness.'
'I've never felt like I deserved happiness.'
'I'm not capable of happiness.'
'I'm afraid to look for happiness because I might fail and look
    foolish.'
'It's too selfish.'
'There's so much suffering and tragedy in the world, what right
    do I have to be happy?'

Next, I want to give you another quality control opportunity, so have a further scan of all your beliefs and weed out the weak or frivolous ones. Often people say they can tell the ones that apply because they react strongly to them. Sometimes they get a sharp feeling in the pit of their stomach, or they might smile in a nervous kind of way, or they become tearful or feel ashamed.

Step Three: Promoting positive beliefs

Now I want you to select two or three of the negative beliefs. On another sheet of paper, draw a line down the middle. On the left side I'd like you to pen in big letters **LIMITING BELIEFS** and list underneath it all the remaining negative attitudes, one after the other.

On the right side at the top of the page write the words **LIBERATING BELIEFS**. The aim of this task now is to help you begin the process of overcoming these negative obstacles by transforming them into positive, constructive, empowering beliefs.

Here's how. Say, in your **LIMITING BELIEFS** column, you wrote down 'Looking for happiness is pointless'. Now scan across to the **LIBERATING BELIEFS** side to reframe this attitude and write down a corresponding but new self-affirming view, such as 'There is a point to happiness as it's been proven to lead to healthier lives'.

When transforming old, obsolete views on happiness into helpful attitudes, it's important that you keep these principles in mind. First, use similar language, as in the example above. I changed 'pointless' into 'there is a point'. Also, your statements should always be phrased using positive language only. The subconscious mind only responds to words written in the affirmative. So, if your negative belief is, 'I'm not the kind of person who deserves happiness', don't replace it with 'I don't deserve to be unhappy'. Instead: 'I deserve happiness'. Finally, the subconscious tends to prefer simple, straightforward language. So there's no need to complicate matters with complex syntax or excessive wordiness such as 'I deserve every bit of happiness that the whole entire world can offer'.

Keep in theme-related. Keep it positive. Keep it simple.

Go through each of your limiting beliefs and transform them all into liberating attitudes. Be sure to write all your new beliefs down in the right-hand column, directly across from the outdated ones. Next, take your pen and physically cross out all the old, outdated beliefs. It's important that you actually scratch out these old views. The subconscious mind is more likely to register 'out with the old, in with the new' if it's reinforced with this gesture.

Step Four: The power of metaphor

When working with the subconscious, there's no use in employing logic or reason. It doesn't work here. The subconscious instead usually prefers to communicate using imagery – think of the power of dream analysis, the cornerstone of Freudian psychotherapy. So, in order to get the message through to our subconscious, to replace the old images with newer ones, we often employ the use of metaphor.

To participate in this aspect of the exercise you will need to find a quiet room, a place where you can remain undisturbed for about twenty minutes or so. Next, I want you first to take a look at the following paragraphs, which represent our metaphor. I often recommend to my clients that they read the passage first, then record it on tape and play it back while they're sitting comfortably in a quiet room. It just makes the process easier. One point to keep in mind, however: if you do opt to record, don't rush through the reading, speak in slow, soothing tones. And be sure to space out some of the words and phrases in accordance with the corresponding physical exercises. Here's the passage:

I'd like you to sit comfortably in a chair, feet a little apart, hands relaxed and falling loosely in your lap. Even though your eyes are closed, keep your head looking forward so as not to strain your neck.

Breathe in deeply through your nose and exhale through your mouth, four times. Very slowly, very relaxed. Breath deeply and evenly.

Now I want you to focus all your attention on your feet and visualise them in your mind without opening your eyes. Once you can picture them, I next want you physically to tense up all the muscles in your feet and visualise yourself as you're doing so. Keep them tense for about five seconds and then slowly relax them. Watch yourself in your mind's eye as you relax.

Next I want you to concentrate on your calves. Imagine

your calves in your mind's eye and physically tense those muscles for about five seconds, visualising yourself as you do so. After about five seconds or so, let these muscles relax. Let all the tension melt away, envisioning your calves as you do so.

Breathe easily and just relax.

Now I want you to concentrate on your thigh muscles. As you sit in the chair, I want you to imagine yourself tensing these muscles as you do so and clench them tightly for about five seconds. And then relax them, and let all the stress and strains just flow away.

Breathe easily and just relax.

Next, I want you to move up to your torso. Focus all your thoughts on this part of the body as you tense it up really tightly. After five seconds, relax and let all the stress and tension flow away.

Now we move up to your shoulders and neck. Tense them up tightly, watching yourself in your mind's eye as you do so. When five seconds pass, relax. Just relax and stay quiet for a few seconds, breathing easily and calmly as you do so.

Now we're going to concentrate on your face and the top of your head. Tense these muscles up very tightly, envisioning these actions as you do so, and after five seconds relax and let all the tension flow away, focusing your thoughts on your face and head as you do so.

Now we're going to focus on your arms and hands. First tense up the top of your arms, then your forearms, and then finally your hands. Tense them up tightly into fists, imagining yourself as you do this. After five seconds, relax your fists, then your forearms, then the top of your arms and let all the tension flow away. Watching yourself in your mind's eye as you do so.

Now that you are in a state of relaxation, I want you to visualise yourself somewhere in the natural world. This could be a forest or a field or maybe a beach. The choice is yours, as long as it's somewhere you feel safe and secure. This is your special place. You feel so comfortable here. So at ease with yourself and the world around you. As you stand there out in nature, you're totally at peace. You've never felt more relaxed, more safe and secure.

As you stand there basking in the calm tranquillity of the scene before you, focus your mind's eye on your surroundings. Concentrate on what you see, focus now on the smells of the scene, now the sounds, now feel the warmth of the sun on your back and the cool, gentle, soothing breeze on your face. You are totally at peace. You're even more relaxed than ever.

Now it's time for a journey. I want you to take a little walk. While still focusing on the peace and calm you feel, and the sights and sounds and smells of your surroundings, you begin your journey and suddenly notice up ahead that there's a little cottage. It's okay to approach this cottage. It's a safe place. It's a good place. Only good things will happen to you here. In fact, the little house is so charming, you look forward to seeing what's inside, so you hurry up the little pathway, open the gate and head up the walkway to the front door. It's a large red door with a big brass knocker right in the centre. You lift up the knocker to announce your arrival, but the door opens on its own. The atmosphere is welcoming, safe and relaxing, so much so that you enter the cottage.

Inside, in the centre of the room, you notice a table. It's okay to approach the table and you walk over to it. There's a big, red leather book resting on top and a golden pen lying next to it. On the cover of this book, written in black letters, you see the words 'My Beliefs'. Go over to the book, pick it up and turn to the first page. Notice the smooth feel of the soft leather as you hold it in your hand.

As you focus all your attention on this page, you suddenly notice that all your old beliefs about happiness are written down. In your mind's eye, pick up the pen that's lying next to the book and first cross out those old beliefs. Cross them out so hard and so vigorously, that the page is covered in ink. So much so, that you can no longer make out any of the words or letters. Once you've done that, I then want you to envision yourself tearing out this page, really imagine yourself as you grip the book and rip it out and tear it to shreds.

As you're standing there holding the crumpled shreds of paper, suddenly you notice a small fire in a fireplace in the corner of the room. Imagine yourself walking over to the fire and throwing these bits of paper into the bright flames. Stand there for a few moments and watch the shreds dissolve into burning embers and finally disappear into ash.

Now you can return to the book on the table. Once again pick up the pen and write down at the top of a fresh page the words 'New Beliefs'. Imagine yourself as you do so, concentrating hard on and taking time over each letter, each word. Next, I want you to put down all your new beliefs about happiness. Write them down slowly. Write them down with great care. Think about each of these new beliefs. Think about what your life is like now that you've got new attitudes about being happy. Think how much more rewarding, much more fulfilling, your life is now and how much better it is to become. Focus on your sense of liberation, confidence, joy and well-being now that the old beliefs are consigned to the ashes in the fireplace. Really magnify, strengthen and enhance those wonderful feelings.

Take a few seconds to do so. Now you can turn around and leave the little cottage. Watch yourself as you walk out of the door. The sun is shining very brightly. The birds are singing very sweetly and the flowers are more fragrant. Your feelings of peace and tranquillity are even greater than before. You're happier within yourself than you've ever thought possible. Enjoy these uplifting, serene and empowering feelings for a few moments.

When you're ready, gently open your eyes. Remain seated for a few more moments and slowly rise from the chair.

This exercise will help reinforce your new beliefs about happiness, but it's only the first step. The subconscious likes to be reminded over and over again of new beliefs before the message gets through permanently.

To strengthen your new attitudes take fifteen or twenty small, round blue sticky labels – office workers often use them to mark out employee holiday time on calendars or colour-code files – and place them throughout your home and office: in kitchen cabinets, desk drawers, wardrobes, filing cabinet at work, in your car. It doesn't really matter where. Every time you come across one of them, however, I want you to take a few seconds to concentrate on your new beliefs about happiness.

NLP: THE ART OF THE POSSIBLE

Of course, the subconscious isn't the only way to change our belief structures. There are many more direct, less wacky, methods at our disposal, too. Starting with Neuro Linguistic Programming, or NLP for short.

I use its principles every day myself and regularly advise my professional and clinical clients to follow suit. The results are amazing and they're so simple to use. Developed originally by a linguist and a computer scientist, NLP, which is akin to CBT, similarly aims to alter our view of the world and transforms even the most negative attitudes into positive and life-enhancing ones. We'll be looking at these principles in more depth throughout the book, but for now here is an introduction.

NLP Principles

1. **The map is not the territory.** This is one of the most effective rules of thumb I can think of for helping to reduce conflict between people. In essence, this principle claims that there are many valid sides to an argument. Conflict often flares up because people get so locked into thinking that there's only ONE solution to a problem (and usually it's their solution), they can't see that someone else might also have a valid viewpoint. After all, there's no written law that only one person can be right. Lots of people can be right, just for different reasons.

   Let's take an example. Suppose a new work colleague canvassed everyone in the office for advice on the best route home. You might suggest the main roads, because they cover the shortest distance from A to B. Another colleague disagrees and instead advises the back roads. The mileage might be a bit more but these streets are less susceptible to traffic jams during peak hours. A third co-worker shakes her head and makes another suggestion. She advises yet another route because it passes the supermarket so they can do their shopping on the way home.

   Who's right? Well, everyone. Once you get into the habit of seeing the validity of an argument from many different perspectives, even if you remained convinced your view is still the strongest, conflict tends to disappear.

2. **We don't make decisions with the benefit of hindsight.**
    Sometimes we make good decisions, other times they're total
    turkeys. Decision-making is not an exact science and,
    occasionally, despite the impressive facts and figures and other
    evidence that's presented to us or that failsafe gut instinct we
    can always rely on, oops, we can still get it wrong. If, with
    hindsight, you realise you made a mistake, there's no need to
    beat yourself up about it. Instead you might want to analyse
    the situation and assess where the decision-making process let
    you down, so that you can learn for next time.

3. **There is no such thing as failure, only feedback.** Fear of
    failure is a great disabler. Probably the greatest. Being afraid
    holds us back and stops us from achieving our goals. Failure's
    a negative word. It serves no purpose whatsoever. So I've
    banished it from my vocabulary and replaced it with feedback.
    When I don't get what I want first time round, I learn from
    the experience and try again.

    Failure is a dead end. We feel bad about ourselves and less
    inclined to venture into new and exciting arenas in the future.
    Feedback, on the other hand, is a transformer. You learn from
    your experience. You didn't get that dream job? No, it doesn't
    mean that you're automatically incapable, useless or
    incompetent. Instead, maybe you need to brush up on your
    skills, get some more experience or sign up for further
    qualifications. The publisher turned down your detective
    novel? Maybe they don't specialise in crime stories and you
    should look around for a publishing house whose speciality is
    this genre, take a class on narrative structure or think about
    turning it into a screenplay. You were so nervous when pitching
    a presentation to potential clients that you stumbled over your
    words, knocked the flipchart over and spilled coffee all over the
    chief exec? Then go on a presentation-training course and stay

away from hot liquids in the boardroom.

If we focus solely on the failure we might never show our faces in public again. If we emphasise the feedback, we come back stronger.

4. **Every cloud has a silver lining.** Most of us at one stage or other have had to deal with difficult, annoying or aggressive people. Maybe it's a bullying boss or a competitive colleague or an interfering relative. The end result? They drive us crazy and cause us sleepless nights.

We're not always in a position to assert our views without fear of reprisals – such as sudden unemployment or the cold shoulder at family reunions – but all is not lost. Whenever you find yourself in one of these situations, try to tease out something positive from it.

It's not as difficult as it sounds and is often quiet empowering. If you're routinely humiliated by a boss or co-worker, then you might want to remind yourself that you would never abuse your own authority and position in this way, or focus instead on how insecure this person must be if they have to resort to bullying. If a colleague is excessively competitive, then maybe they're helping you raise the standard and quality of your own work. If your mother constantly criticises your appearance, complains about your lack of love life or criticises your messy house, then maybe she's really afraid of no longer feeling needed. The point is this: we can't always change our situation, shun relatives or send our boss to charm school. However, finding something positive about these disagreeable encounters helps restore some equilibrium to our self-esteem.

5. **If at first you don't succeed, try something different.** Sometimes when we're trying to solve our problems we become stuck and rely on using the same strategy over and

over again. Even if it doesn't work! You look for a job through the newspaper, and ignore all other sources of employment – recruitment agencies, the internet, networking, family and friends, job centre. You go to clubs to find a new mate, and don't even give a second thought to introduction by friends, personal ads, dating agencies, social clubs or the internet. In short, keep your options open and your strategies flexible.

Exercise 16:
Exploring NLP

I want you to use the first NLP rule (**The map is not the territory**) and set up a behavioural experiment using this principle. Perhaps you're constantly locking horns with someone at work, or maybe you and an acquaintance or relative never quite seem to be on the same wave length, or perhaps you and your partner can never see eye to eye on a particular domestic point. The situation itself is not important.

With this NLP rule in mind, I want you to try to look at a source of conflict from someone else's viewpoint and then notice your own thoughts, feelings and behaviours when you interact with this person. Do you view him or her differently? Did you approach the conversation differently? How was your manner during this exchange? How did the other person react to you? Were different conclusions reached? Most people have told me that they feel less anxious and that tensions seem to ease up during subsequent exchanges.

HAPPINESS MYTH #3:
INTELLIGENT PEOPLE ARE HAPPIER THAN
THOSE WITH LOW IQs

Although intelligence is highly prized in the Western world and often associated with successful, interesting and more prestigious jobs, higher salaries and enhanced social status, the evidence suggests that it is completely unconnected to happiness.

WEEK FIVE:

Moving Towards Change

Welcome to the fifth week. We're more than halfway through the program now. Take a few moments to reflect on your progress over the past few weeks. What stands out most in your mind? What's been the most helpful? What real changes and improvements have you noticed? What areas do you still need to work on?

As usual, there are a few tasks and activities from the previous weeks that I'm going to ask you to keep doing. They are:

1. Looking after your health
2. Thirty minutes of physical exercise three times a week
3. Ten to fifteen minutes' relaxation every day
4. Improving sleep
5. Mirror exercise
6. Random acts of smiling
7. Exchanging good news
8. Thirty minutes a week on your hobby
9. Blue dot exercise

This week, we're going to be concentrating on some of the different areas in your life where you'd like to make improvements and focus on ways to make these changes happen. We do this through formulating and setting goals.

Our aims and ambitions are crucial to our well-being, whether it's a question of planning our day-to-day activities or anticipating the future. CBT can help us organise our day efficiently or inspire us to make huge, sweeping changes.

EXERCISE 17:
REWARDING YOURSELF FOR
ALL YOUR HARD WORK

Before we begin looking at goal-setting strategies, I think first you deserve some recognition for your hard work and commitment to this program. Without a taster of the gain, where's the joy? Where's the incentive to continue?

If you're the type of person who rarely pampers yourself, now's the time to start. You deserve it. This is not mere indulgence, I promise. Psychologically speaking, people are much more likely to maintain their levels of motivation if they reward themselves for their hard work (remember positive reinforcement?). So, your first task of week five is to go out and treat yourself. You don't have to break the bank or spend hour upon hour, but I do want you to do something special just for you. Update your image with a new haircut or splurge on a new outfit. Relax with a facial or massage. How about that new restaurant that's met with rave reviews, or maybe indulge yourself with a box of Belgian chocolates? It's entirely up to you. And not just this week, every week. No buts. No negative thoughts. No critical inner voice. Just enjoy.

EXERCISE 18:
FORMULATING GOALS

Now it's back to work. Let's start thinking about setting some goals. Although goal formulation and targeting is central to our happiness and well-being, the process can be a little on the complex side. It's not difficult, it just requires some organisation.

Step One: Conceiving goals

One way to increase your personal satisfaction is by first exploring the different areas of your life and thinking about possible avenues for change. Once you identify and prioritise these target areas, they then form the basis of goals.

Why is this important? Not only are goals the first step towards making real improvements in our lives – after all, if you can't name it, you can't claim it – but scientists have actually discovered that a part of our brain, called the cingulate nucleus, becomes stimulated under two conditions: pre-goal attainment happiness and post-goal attainment happiness. In other words, the mere acts of formulating and achieving goals actually make us feel good.

So, I'd like you to do the following exercise. You'll have to set aside between thirty minutes to an hour of undisturbed time to complete it all. Some people prefer to do it in two stages and that's okay too.

First, get hold of ten blank sheets of paper. Then write down the following ten categories, one on each page.

1. Career
2. Relationships
3. Health and fitness
4. Education

5. Travel and adventure
6. Spirituality
7. Me
8. Finances
9. Personal development
10. Recreation

Next, stand up and spread out the sheets of paper on the floor, so they surround you. Take a few moments and just think about each of these categories one at a time, focusing on how they impact on your life. Which ones are you happy with? Which make you feel unhappy?

Once you've done that, I'd like you then to go and stand on, and I mean physically step on, the category that represents your greatest desire for change and improvement.

Let's take career as an example. Many people claim that their current job makes them unhappy and this is not surprising. Having a career you find stimulating and rewarding is a major factor in happiness. After all, we spend at least forty hours a week, if not more, working at our job. That's a lot of time for someone who's unhappy. So, as you stand on the sheet marked career, I'd like you really to reflect and concentrate on your current job situation. In what ways are you happy with your work? How are you unhappy? Maybe you've been in the same position for far too long. Perhaps it was only ever meant to be a temporary post, and you've ended up staying longer than you anticipated. Would you like something more challenging? Do you like your current field, but feel it's time for promotion? Or perhaps you'd like to switch careers entirely.

Now concentrate on the year ahead. How would you like to improve your work situation over the next twelve months? What steps could you take to achieve this? Perhaps you could put out feelers to people who already work in this industry to find out what further qualifications and experience you'd need. I bet they'd even give you the lowdown – the good points and the bad – so you could rule out any 'grass is always greener' scenarios. Or perhaps you're quite happy with your present company, just not satisfied with the job itself. So you might want to pay a visit to the human resources office and see what other positions are available.

After you've wracked your brain along these lines for a little while, pick up that piece of paper and write 'first priority'. You might also want to jot down any other ideas and thoughts that popped into your mind.

Once you've given your career sufficient attention, it's then time to move on to your next priority area for change. So, look around at the remaining scattered sheets of paper at your feet and identify goal number two. Carry on in this manner until you've prioritised and completed all ten categories. Of course, you might find you only really want to make changes in one or two areas of your life or perhaps there are other areas of prime importance to you that I haven't identified here. Feel free to tailor-make this exercise. It's about your needs after all.

Step Two: Believable goals

Far be it for me to be a wet blanket or intentionally rain on anyone's parade, but . . . Now that you've identified your goal target areas, we have to consider a reality check. Your ambitions have to be realistic because if they're not you'll just be setting yourself up for disappointment, failure and frustration.

It's all very well and good to aspire to centre court at Wimbledon, but in all honesty how likely is this prospect if you're fifty-five and have never even picked up a tennis racket before? Probably not very.

However, if you've worked as a secretary in a law firm for going on ten years and have always harboured hidden aspirations of being a legal eagle yourself, then what's stopping you? People switch careers all the time. Why not you?

Just be honest with yourself and be realistic. Be frank about your abilities, your financial situation and the other resources at your disposal. Do you know what achieving your goal entails? Do you have the stamina to juggle responsibilities? Are you the type who caves in under pressure?

Address these points and you'll have your answer.

Step Three: Achieving goals

Long-term goals

There's something to be said for those courageous souls who throw caution to the wind, take the plunge and just go for it. Once they've got a goal in mind, they're off and running. Without so much as a backward glance.

But not everyone is so brave (or impulsive, depending how you look at it) when it comes to making radical changes. In fact, most of us find such abrupt behaviour far too daunting and prefer to adopt a slower, more thoughtful pace. There's also a lot to be said for taking your time and proceeding carefully. Besides, you might not be in any position to up sticks and chase your dreams in such a spontaneous way. Mortgages. Children. Pets. Payments. All pretty good reasons not to act rashly. Remember, this isn't a race. Achieve your goals at your own pace.

One of the best ways to achieve long-term goals and maintain motivation during the long haul is to break them down into a series of smaller, more manageable sub-targets. In psychology, we call this process chunking. If you feel overwhelmed by the prospect of spending several years of your life training to achieve your dream of becoming a surgeon, you can learn to appreciate the small achievements along the way. Getting accepted into medical school.

Passing first-year exams. Graduating. Obtaining your first hospital job. Focusing on these mini-targets will give you a constant sense of achievement and help keep you focused.

Let's play around with this concept for a while. I want you to dig out those ten sheets of paper where you just listed your priorities and choose the first three. If you've changed your mind and want to re-prioritise any of these goals, then feel free to do so. Next, take a blank sheet of paper and divide it into three equal sections. At the top of the left-hand column, I want you to jot down the word 'goals'. In the middle, please write 'five years', then finish off by putting 'ten years' in the final column.

Now, refer back to each of your three goals and list them separately, one after the other, underneath the 'goals' column. Next, consider each of these ambitions in turn and decide where you'd like to be in five years' and then ten years' time. Write your answers down in the appropriate column. Your paper should look something like this.

Goals	Five years	Ten years
Advertising career	Account executive	Partner
Family	Married	Birth of first child
Property	Starter house	Bigger house

Medium-term goals

Tables like these are useful because they help you visualise the path and direction of your goals. Your medium-term plans are essential to this process because achieving them means you'll be that much closer to your ultimate dream. In other words, they keep you on track. Since medium-term goals are targets in their own right, you might also want to think about drawing a similar diagram. Here, instead, you could mark the columns: 'goals', 'three years' and 'five years'.

Weekly goals

Even with the best will and intentions in the world, it's not always easy to maintain high levels of motivation and enthusiasm to achieve our goals – especially if the final dream looms somewhere in the dim and distant future. To keep yourself motivated and focused, I recommend that you set aside a section in your weekly calendar to list any tasks required for the long-haul goals. And stick to them.

So, if your ambition is to be an interior designer then even very early on there's plenty you can do to get you started on this pathway. You'll want to contact college admissions departments about entry requirements. You might have to take some more exams in preparation for enrolment. By organising your time in this way, and ensuring you stick to these weekly goals, you keep your dream, distant though it may be, fresh in your mind.

Daily goals

Organising our thoughts and planning in this way is useful too for meeting our day-to-day commitments and responsibilities. We have to address our more immediate goals, not just concentrate on the long-term aims. So I also recommend taking a few minutes, either when you first get into work in the morning or maybe even the night before, to give some thought to the day ahead. Here's how.

Step One: Start off by brainstorming and jotting down everything you need to accomplish that day. The urgent, the unimportant, the enjoyable, the trivial. Write it all down in a list. Whatever springs to mind.

Step Two: Once you've finished, it's then time to begin prioritising your daily goals. Go to the top of the list and give each item one of the following rankings. A is for those tasks that have to be completed by the end of the day. B represents less urgent demands. They're still important, just not crucial. And the Cs can be consigned to another day.

Step Three: Now group the items together by letter, and then taking each cluster individually, repeat the ranking process once more. In other words, take the A group and rate the most important task A1, the next most urgent A2, and so on.

Step Four: This final step is very important. As you proceed through your day and accomplish all the goals on your list, make sure you cross them out. Pick up your pen and physically draw a line through each completed task. This action, signifying completion, actually sends a signal to the brain. The cingulate nucleus then becomes activated, signifying post-goal attainment, which is why we feel a sense of happiness from achieving our goals. But you have to write them down and cross them off. Merely 'doing' is not enough.

EXERCISE 19:
THE SECOND NLP PRINCIPLE

Your final task this week is to incorporate the second NLP principle (**We don't make decisions with the benefit of hindsight**) somewhere in your life. Maybe you have a big decision looming this week at work or at home and are really torn between two options. So much so, you're stressed because you're unsure what to do. You could try writing down all the advantages and disadvantages of each possibility. Maybe you could confide in someone whose advice you respect and trust. Although many people feel embarrassed to ask for help in these situations, as if it somehow reflects negatively on their ability to make sound judgements, I think it shows responsibility. We can't know everything and other people can be invaluable as sounding boards. You should also think about the various outcomes of each option and consider worst-case scenario strategies and solutions. This is very important because should the proverbial hit the fan during a crisis, your reputation among your colleagues will really soar if you are able to demonstrate a cool head and a way of resolving the crisis.

Even if you don't have any major decisions to make in the near future, you might want to think about the judgements you've exercised in the past. Especially a situation in which, with hindsight, you might have chosen a different course of action. Maybe a really exciting career opportunity cropped up, but you declined it because you felt the job was too challenging for your level of experience. A few days later you changed your mind, but by then it was too late. Your colleague with even less experience had gladly accepted it! Or maybe you chose Mr/Ms A, when Mr/Ms B turned out too late to be the right one all along.

We all have regrets, but beating ourselves up over our decisions is not the answer. Painful or disappointing these experiences may be, but we can learn from them for next time. In the case of the premature job offer, the solution might be as simple as asking for a few days before giving an answer. That way you have some space and can calmly consider the requirements for the post in light of your experience. In terms of disastrous relationship choices, ask yourself what qualities you want in your choice of mate (and those you don't want!) and steer clear of those who don't measure up.

Happiness Myth No. 4:
Money makes us happy

While money can buy us big houses, expensive cars, gorgeous designer clothes, it can't guarantee us happiness.

Bad news for Lottery winners, good news for everyone else . . . studies have shown that winning a fortune, despite the increased financial status, has no positive impact on people's mood in the long run, surprising as that might seem. In fact, unforeseen problems tend to arise, causing new worries and burdens. Following a windfall, Lottery winners complain their friends treat them differently, they lose their social network after giving up their job, and marriages sometimes collapse under the strain.

Overcoming Doubts and Setbacks

GETTING ENERGISED, REVITALISED AND BACK ON TRACK

Let's begin week six in the usual manner. Take a few moments to think about all the exercises you have done so far and the program in general. In what ways has your life improved? What have you found most helpful? What areas do you still need to work on?

As always, I'd like you to carry on with some of the previous tasks and activities:

1. Looking after your health
2. Thirty minutes of physical exercise at least three times a week
3. Ten to fifteen minutes' relaxation every day
4. Improving sleep
5. Mirror exercises
6. Random acts of smiling
7. Exchanging good news
8. Thirty minutes a week on your hobby
9. Blue dot exercise
10. Keep up with daily task list

The theme of the next seven days is remotivation. It's often about this time in a program that attention levels begin to flag or unsettling recurrences of doubt or negativity set in. This is not unusual. In fact, it's perfectly normal for previous obstacles and niggling anxieties to resurface during any kind of intensive, demanding program like this one.

Striving for happiness takes effort and hard work, despite all the amazing benefits it brings. You've already passed that all-important halfway mark. You're coming up to the 'sixth-week blues', and unless we explore them a little further, you might lose motivation, concentration and dedication. So let's get things back on track.

EXERCISE 20:
ADDRESSING THE NEGATIVE

Right at the beginning of this book I mentioned that it's not uncommon for people to feel paradoxically unhappy or unsettled at some point during this program. Take a few moments now to think about your own emotions. What feelings and thoughts, both positive and negative, have come to the fore since you started it?

Personal improvement isn't always easy or smooth. Even when we set out to make positive changes in our life, it's normal sometimes for upsetting memories and emotions to emerge. So, don't worry. It's not a setback. As you know by now, negative feelings serve a purpose. Sometimes people no longer feel the need to bury and suppress their unpleasant emotions and this release is part of a cathartic and healing process. For others, the expression of these pent-up emotions is a bit like shedding an old skin. As people emerge from the obsolete chrysalis and face new challenges the unknown can sometimes seem very daunting. Suddenly the old and familiar starts looking more attractive and it's tempting to revert to former habits and modes of thought. But by this stage people have often outgrown their former beliefs and behaviours, so even if they retreat into this comfort zone, the former life will no longer be as satisfying. Still others sometimes feel regret that they've waited so long to make these beneficial changes to their lives. Finally, for some, the demands of this course can sometimes cause pressure, especially if they clash with other commitments. It's easy to feel over-burdened and drained. As with any program of study, it's not uncommon to wonder occasionally if the ultimate benefits are worth the stress.

These hurdles are normal and temporary. People usually resolve them quickly. After a day or two they find they're able to purge their anxieties and 'get them out of their system'. Immediately they feel a hundred times better for doing so. Or they're able to strike a more balanced, realistic approach to co-ordinating the course commitments and their other responsibilities. The result? Since they begin to notice real positive changes occurring they're more motivated than ever to continue.

However, if you do feel unduly overwhelmed or churned up inside, maybe you should step back a pace or two. Take two weeks instead of one to complete the tasks and requirements. Think about how you might be able to delegate some of your other responsibilities to family members or work colleagues. At the beginning of every week, devise a feasible schedule so that you can organise and plan your personal and program commitments.

EXERCISE 21:
WHAT'S SO BAD ABOUT BEING YOU?

Maybe for you the personal issues raised aren't about times pressures at all. Maybe it's back to old problems of low self-esteem, despite sticking to the program. Just remember, many people feel despondent about themselves, even when they're on the path to self-improvement. What's worse, they often zero in on their least desirable personality traits and entirely ignore their positive qualities. Because of these lopsided negative self-perceptions, their self-esteem takes a battering. So much so, they convince themselves they're not capable or deserving of a better life.

If this sounds familiar, take heart. This is real CBT textbook stuff. Most of us dislike at least one or two of our characteristics, but happy people either accept their human limitations or try to change those they don't like.

What are your self-defeating attitudes? Would you like to take the first steps to transform them? Here's how. Find some paper and go to a quiet room where you won't be disturbed or interrupted for about fifteen minutes. On the left-hand side of the page, jot down the words 'List One'; underneath, I want you to write down seven adjectives which in your mind best describe how you feel about yourself right now – positive and negative. Once you've written them all down, take a few more moments and think carefully about your choice of descriptions. Feel free to make any changes if something more appropriate springs to mind.

Many people list emotion words like, sad, lonely, resentful, angry, anxious, guilty or unappreciated. Others also refer to more general descriptions such as educated, sexual, dedicated, loving, friendly, shy, extroverted, fair-minded, creative, caring or protective.

Once you've finished, take a look at the words you've chosen to describe yourself. Do you really want to feel this way about yourself? What changes would you like to make?

If you're dissatisfied with any aspects of your personality or current situation, then you can begin to think about making changes. On the right-hand side of your first list, I want you to create a second one and label it 'List Two'. This time, however, I want you to take any negative, self-defeating adjectives from List

One and transform them into traits that are positive and self-affirming. Like this:

List One	List Two
Isolated	Sociable
Pessimistic	Optimistic
Anxious	Calm
Chaotic	Organised
Indecisive	Focused
Tired	Energetic
Humourless	Fun

Your next step is to think about your choice of words in List Two. Taking each new trait in turn, I want you to spend a few moments visualising what this life would be like for you. What would it be like to embody this kind of person? How would your life be different? What would you be able to achieve that you can't do now? How would these new beliefs make you happy? What changes would you need to make to become this person? What steps would you need to take?

EXERCISE 22:
OVERCOMING BLOCKS

The exercise you've just taken is brilliant for helping you identify and transform your self-defeating beliefs. Your former limiting attitudes only fuel your unhappiness, so good riddance to them. Now that you've made serious inroads towards changing yourself for the better on a conscious level, let's reinforce your new resolve for happiness by appealing to the subconscious.

You'll need to find a quiet room where you'll be left

undisturbed for about twenty minutes. Take a look at the following passages and, if you find it helpful, you might want to record it on your cassette player. As you read it, make sure your voice is calm and soothing; don't rush through the words or become distracted by the sound of your voice on tape.

Sit in a comfortable chair, legs uncrossed, eyes closed, head straight and hands and arms falling loosely to your sides or on your lap. Imagine you find yourself outside one morning, walking in a beautiful forest. You are overcome by the most amazing sense of peace, safety and tranquillity as you walk through the trees. In fact, you've never felt more secure, more at peace, more relaxed, in your life.

As you walk around the forest, focus on the sights you see: the trees, the mountains in the distance, the little stream rushing past your feet. Imagine what it's like to feel the earth beneath your feet, to smell the fresh air, to hear the birds singing happily in the trees. Again, you are at total peace and feel very, very safe, secure and relaxed here in this beautiful forest.

You're feeling so safe and so relaxed, you begin to walk further afield through the forest. Suddenly you're struck by your strong feelings of happiness as you remember your new beliefs about yourself, about being happy and achieving your other goals in life. As you walk through the forest, out of the corner of your eye you spy a blue dot on one of the trees and this reminder reinforces your new beliefs and your feelings of safety, relaxation and well-being.

As you're walking around and thinking these happy thoughts, all of a sudden, through a clearing in the trees, you notice a little old woman, sitting on a tree stump ahead. She notices you, too, and gets up and starts to approach you. The old woman looks very unhappy. She has a big scowl on her face, but you can tell she wishes you no harm. In fact, her aim is to protect you from disappointment and despair and keep you well.

You greet this woman and say hello and quite confidently tell her all about your new beliefs about happiness. This woman is sceptical and shakes her head dismissively. She thinks it's safer for you to hold on to your outdated beliefs. She tells you why she thinks your new beliefs are wrong. She tells you that happiness won't last, you'll only end up feeling let down, or that you're selfish for pursuing happiness in the first place.

As you stand there together, with the old woman rattling off her list of reasons why you shouldn't pursue happiness, you find your own resolve to achieve this goal getting stronger and stronger. Each time the old woman gives you a negative reason you smile brightly at her and inform her firmly that you no longer hold those unhelpful, outdated beliefs. Now you truly believe that life is full of happiness and joy, and happiness is something you deserve. Speak with conviction and let her know how deeply felt are your new beliefs. Tell her assertively, but kindly, that nothing she can say will make you change your mind. Thank her for her concern and tell her she no longer needs to protect you in this way. She smiles at you and nods her head, convinced that your new beliefs serve you well. She knows she no longer has to protect you from disappointment. You smile in return, wish her happiness and say goodbye. Turn around and walk along the path, feeling strong, secure and full of total happiness as you go.

Sit there in your chair for a few moments and bask in the peace, relaxation and total happiness you now feel. Really magnify these feelings inside yourself. When you are ready, open your eyes.

Once you've opened your eyes, take a few moments to think about your new thoughts and feelings about happiness. Do you feel more energised? More committed to your goal of happiness?

EXERCISE 23:
THE THIRD NLP PRINCIPLE

Your next task this week is to think about the third NLP principle. (**There's no such thing as failure, only feedback**), applying it to your own life. Maybe at one point in the past you summoned up the nerve to try something courageous, only to be disappointed by the result. Perhaps you approached a veritable god or goddess, only to be shot down dismissively. Or there might have been an interview for a fantastic job, but you were so nervous you could barely speak and just ended up wishing the ground would swallow you up.

We've all been there. We've all had occasions where we failed to shine or disastrous encounters that left us scampering away, tail between our legs, licking our wounds in humiliation. However, although it's tempting to lodge these experiences away in the 'no way, never again, no more risks' category of our brain, the strongest, happiest, most successful people know that even the most personally soul-destroying circumstances are invaluable and promote positive change. You can learn from these experiences and come back stronger. Once you stop viewing these experiences as failures but reframe them as feedback, there's no stopping you.

Here's an example from my own life. A few years ago, I decided to write a play. I've always been involved in theatre, and one day finally decided, right, it's time to put pen to paper. After a week or two, my fast-paced comedy set in a mental-health clinic was born.

Although I was briefed by my thesp and writing friends that

the theatrical world was in a huge financial crisis and forced to rely on the toe-tapping musical favourites of yesteryear just to keep commercially afloat (in other words, unknown first-time playwrights need not apply), I remained steadfastly optimistic and undeterred. I must have sent my play to close to one hundred theatre companies and the feedback, if I received any at all, was invariably the same. 'Thanks, but definitely no thanks.'

Not only did they not jump at the chance to stage my play, on the rare occasion I did receive any kind of genuine feedback for my efforts, I was firmly advised not to give up the day job. Ouch! Yes, their scathing rejections were upsetting and my ego was bruised at first. However, once I got over the lack of enthusiasm for my work, I sat down and looked at the play objectively. Through their eyes. And, in truth, my comedy wasn't good enough. Not by a long shot.

As luck would have it, I became acquainted with a professional producer-playwright-director who had been affiliated with the RSC. This man sat me down and explained all the many reasons why my play wasn't currently up to scratch and gave me suggestions on how to make improvements. Furthermore, he said if I made those changes, he'd even consider staging it himself at Stratford. In short, I did. He did. My comedy premiered in August 2000 to rave reviews. There's no greater thrill than attending the opening night for your own play, I can assure you.

The theatrical world is rife with rejection. And, yes, I could have caved in to the hurt and humiliation of writing a duff play. But I didn't. I believed it had potential and set about trying to find ways to make the necessary improvements. Viewing this experience as feedback, instead of failure, helped me achieve this very important goal.

I did it. You can too. So your task now is to think back over your life and visualise a situation in which you feel you failed, subjected yourself to ridicule or made a serious blunder. Now, as uncomfortable as it might be, think about the negative thoughts and emotions you experienced as a result of this so-called disaster. Guilt, embarrassment, shame, anxiety, rejection and loss of confidence tend to be common reactions. Next, think about how this event affected your subsequent behaviour. Were you less likely to take risks? Did you vow never to speak to strangers again? Did you decide to stay in the same tedious job? Did you withdraw from people around you? Did you abandon a dream?

I wouldn't be surprised. The fear of failure is so potent in our society that most of us would prefer to remain unhappy, unfulfilled and stuck than to seek out potentially rewarding, exciting opportunities. So, now, I want you to think about your own example again, but this time focus on what you learned from that experience. Maybe instead of vowing never to approach another attractive member of the same or opposite sex, you can speak to a mutual friend or arrange a group outing. Perhaps the next time you go for a job interview, you'll take more time to prepare. Investigate the company. Think about your own experience in relation to the position. Be honest with yourself about your skills. The feedback perspective might not take the sting out of past humiliations or disappointments, but it can certainly prevent them from happening again.

THE FLIP SIDE

The next exercises for this week both focus on 'reflecting'. As you're aware by now, activity, usually in the guise of a challenging behavioural experiment, is central to the CBT approach and is essential for helping you develop happiness. The same can be said for reflecting. They're really two sides of the same coin, because it's only in thinking about our actions and making corresponding changes to our behaviours that we develop healthier, happier views about ourselves and others.

EXERCISE 24:
WRITE YOUR OWN OBITUARY

This exercise might sound morbid, but it's one of the most helpful ways I know to help people assess their lives and forge their future plans. So, bear with me.

It's vital for all of us as people evolving creatively and spiritually to live a full life before we die. This means being open to new world views and opportunities. This means taking on new challenges and daring to dream. This means gaining strength from adversity and believing in yourself, even in the face of doubt and derision.

When the poet John Betjeman was on the brink of death, what were his last thoughts? Did he wish he'd led a happier life? A more successful one? Been hailed as the most profound poetic voice of our time? No. Betjeman's main regret was that he hadn't had enough sex.

Does this surprise you? Shouldn't a great mind mourn greater, more resonant and profound regrets? Not according to the nineteenth-century existentialist philosopher, Kierkegaard. He argued that when people are lying on their death beds, they're hardly likely to fret about the state of the world, society's ills, politics, art, injustices, pollution or crime. They usually think about their own life, their achievements, potential realised, opportunities missed. With Betjeman it was sex.

So now it's time for you to think about *your* life. Imagine you've been transported through time and are coming to the end of your days.

How would you like to be remembered?
In what ways were you truly 'alive'?
Did you have a passion for life?
Did you wake up feeling enthusiastic about the day ahead?
How would you describe yourself?

What was your major achievement in life?

What were your values?

What sacrifices did you have to make?

What were your most lovable qualities?

In what ways did you make a real difference?

What were the important lessons you learned out of life?

What do you want to be remembered for?

What have you left behind on this planet?

What would you do over again?

What would you have liked to have done?

What would be your words of advice to those left behind on this planet?

What is your biggest regret?

What would you like your epitaph to say?

Once you've thought about these questions and how they relate to your life, you can begin writing your obituary. I usually recommend a paragraph or page, but you can write as much as you like. This exercise is about tapping into your thoughts and feelings about your life, so don't get bogged down in trying to get the style just right. If it's helpful, you can turn to the obituary section of your local newspaper and use their column as a template.

After you've finished take a few minutes to think about the goals and dreams you haven't accomplished yet. What else would you like to achieve in your life?

EXERCISE 25:
THE FOURTH NLP PRINCIPLE

Your final task for the week is to think about the fourth principle NLP (**Every cloud has a silver lining**) and try to envision ways in which it could improve your life.

Wouldn't it be good if, whenever we're confronted with someone nasty, we could just pull out a trusty magic wand and, with a wave of our hand, make them disappear? Puff! Problem sorted.

Reality, of course, is very different. We have little choice but to rely on our ability to limit conflict and use our people skills.

Call to mind a difficult relationship you currently have, perhaps a belittling line manager, unsupportive relative, or excessively competitive co-worker. One that causes you distress. Think about the last time you encountered this person. What was this encounter like? How did you feel? Powerless? Humiliated? Angry? Tense? Insecure?

Now, thinking about this same situation, I want you to identify something positive relating to this exchange. Maybe you yourself are not the type of person to humiliate someone else. But perhaps the other person is so insecure, the only way they can deal with someone else is through insulting them. Maybe you even feel sorry for someone with such inadequate social skills. By shifting focus in this way, you can take back some control. How would you feel then? How will you feel the next time you meet this person?

Let's take Joshua as an example. He was a client of mine who was a highly successful lawyer, devoted husband and caring parent. You couldn't have met a nicer, more responsible man. His father, however, seemed to hold different views. Despite Joshua's numerous fine qualities and achievements, his dad had a tendency to belittle him at every turn. He wasn't making enough money. His wife was nothing special.

Joshua had real difficulties standing up for himself, and his father's endless criticism really used to upset him. For several weeks he and I explored this toxic relationship and it was a painful process for him, because for his whole life he'd wanted nothing more than his father's approval. One of the first steps we took was to employ this principle. I asked him to list three positive aspects of these demeaning encounters, to counterbalance their negative effects. Joshua listed: 1) I know my dad only wants the best for me and to encourage me to live up to my full potential. His heart's in the right place, even though I'd prefer him to express himself in a more supportive way; 2) men of his generation were raised by different standards. They weren't so open with their emotions as we are now and it's not fair of me to judge him by my generation's standards; 3) I have a very loving relationship with my son and I would never belittle him.

Were these three positive aspects a substitute for long-term therapy? No. But they were effective and helped get Joshua through some very sticky and uncomfortable moments with his father while we addressed the more deep-seated, underlying relationship problems in therapy.

HAPPINESS MYTH NO. 5:
MEN ARE HAPPIER THAN WOMEN

There is a widespread, lingering belief that men are naturally much happier than women. Low status, poor wages, difficulties coping in the face of adversity, hormones, you name it, women are still seen as feeble, fragile creatures who dissolve at the first hint of upset. Men, on the other hand, are thought to cope better when trouble strikes. Not true. Women tend to talk more about their problems and express their emotions when upset. Men on the other hand are more likely to anaesthetise their problems through drink or drugs or picking fights.

Learning How to Cope

Welcome to week seven. Predictably, I'd like you to start by taking a few moments to review your progress. How are you getting on? What positive changes are you noticing about yourself? How about in the world around you? What information or exercise is helping you most? What areas do you still need to work on?

As usual, I'd like you to keep up with some tasks and activities:

1. Looking after your health
2. Thirty minutes of physical exercise at least three times per week
3. Ten to fifteen minutes' relaxation every day
4. Improving sleep
5. Mirror exercises
6. Random acts of smiling
7. Exchanging good news
8. Thirty minutes a week on your hobby
9. Blue dot exercise
10. Keep up with daily task list
11. Take time to reflect

FACING UP TO DISASTER

The overall theme of the next couple of weeks is developing effective coping mechanisms so that you will be equipped to handle any future situation, no matter how rocky, disabling, unsteady, stressful, terrifying or nerve-wracking it might be. In CBT, coping skills are synonymous with balanced, rational thought processes.

I've already touched on the five interlinked CBT factors: how our social situations, thoughts, feelings, behaviours and physical sensations all have strong influences on our mind and body. So, if you're harbouring angry feelings about a stressful situation, it's a safe bet you're also entertaining corresponding thoughts, behaviours and physical symptoms. Since it's not always appropriate, desirable or necessary to change the circumstances that cause us unhappiness, we can instead build up stronger coping strategies to help us weather our rockier moments.

With CBT, it's healthy thoughts that make healthy bodies, minds and souls. They are the roots and cornerstones of our emotional state – in other words, it's not so much a case of mind over matter, as mind determining matter. The next two weeks will be devoted to helping you develop further positive and constructive beliefs about yourself and the world around you.

We've already talked about how our subjective interpretations of personal situations and encounters influence the way we think, feel and behave in response, and that thoughts aren't automatically facts. Our earlier discussions of CBT were, however, just the introductory lecture. Now you're ready for the master class. Irrational thoughts: the heart and soul of CBT.

While it's not faulty thoughts that cause our emotional pain, they are a central factor in perpetuating our distress. If we can first learn to identify our negative thoughts, or 'sinking feeling', we are in a better position to stop ourselves from feeling worse and, furthermore, make ourselves feel a lot better. The key is that once these thoughts have been identified, we should assess the truthfulness and accuracy of the attitudes they embody, and learn to construct a more balanced and healthy viewpoint.

Let's get the process rolling. It's literally as easy as ABC – as Albert Ellis pointed out. **A** refers to an event or situation that **activates** our emotionally painful response. **B** describes our faulty, unrealistic, perhaps over-hasty **beliefs** about ourselves, other people and the world around us, while **C** stands for the **consequences** of our emotional thinking; in other words, the way we act, feel and respond (again, just because something's a thought, it doesn't make it a fact).

Here's an example of what I mean.

Suppose after several bad runs in the relationship stakes, Cupid's arrow strikes and you finally find the person you want to spend the rest of your life with. You're besotted, you're thrilled. So much so that after only two dates, you've already begun planning the wedding and naming your 3.4 children and 2.5 cats. Sadly, however, love's young dream was not meant to be this time around. Once again you find yourself alone.

When a relationship ends the anguish can be excruciating. Throughout time, poets and writers have waxed lyrical about the pain of unrequited love and broken hearts. Without wishing to minimise the distress suffered, however, it's important to keep our thoughts in perspective and our feelings in check. Not only will the misery fade in time (remember, homeostasis), but also this unpleasant experience connects us with just about everyone else in the human race. Most people, at some point in their life, have been rejected, undermined or rendered emotionally vulnerable by someone important to them. But these very people mostly heal their pain and go on to form lasting, meaningful and fulfilling relationships with others. It may be hell at the time, but it's a temporary hell.

When you're going through a break-up, your thoughts,

actions and behaviours are likely to be coloured by strong and distressing emotions. How do you respond? How does such a break-up affect your view of yourself? How does it impact on the way you see others?

Option A: The healthy reaction

At first, after a break-up, you're probably feeling more than a bit dazed, not quite sure what's happened. Maybe even hoping the goodbye scene was all just a bad dream and you'll wake up one morning with your beloved beside you, or else that the person will call you up berating themselves for being such a fool and begging you to take them back.

However, gradually and painfully, you finally face up to the truth and come to accept that the relationship is over. After a few weeks and months, you slowly begin to pick up the pieces of your life. You're probably still feeling vulnerable and emotionally bruised, but you're no longer crying through the night or relying on comfort food quite so much. You throw yourself into your work as a means of coping. You socialise with your friends. And even if, sometimes, it feels like you're just going through the motions, you keep yourself busy.

After a few more weeks or months, you realise that life is beginning to look a little brighter. Your self-esteem and confidence might still need some boosting but you find yourself spontaneously smiling and laughing much more than you have been lately. You've become your 'old self' again. You look forward to an upcoming jaunt with your friends. You can even begin to see some of the flaws in Mr/Ms Perfect, the ones your friends have been pointing out for months. You then begin to think about all the traits you want and need in a new potential partner. And you start to think hmmm, that new person at work seems awfully nice. What if . . .?

Option B: The unhealthy reaction

Option A doesn't always happen, however. There's the unhealthy flipside, Option B, which is vastly more distressing and painful. Here's how it might go. Even after several months, maybe years, you can't quite accept the relationship is over. Every morning you wake up and feel a sharp stab of pain that this person, this ideal god/goddess, has left you in the lurch and has no plans to come back. Your whole world has collapsed after the break-up and you wonder how or if you'll ever recover. Even with the passing of time, you still feel shattered and traumatised. Try as you might, you can't stop crying, your moods are all over the place, you've lost your appetite and drink and smoke more than you should to block out the pain. Everywhere you go, you see something or someone that reminds you of your beloved. Your favourite restaurant, your song on the radio, the film you saw together. You just haven't been able to move on. Even though the last few months of your relationship were rife with arguments and tears, you still cling to the hope that s/he is coming back. You miss them. You miss their voice. You might even take to calling them up when they're at work just to hear it on their answering machine.

Finally, however, you reluctantly, grudgingly, accept the relationship is over. But instead of moving on, you become angry and bitter, or reticent and afraid, as you vow never, ever again to fall in love or let someone else close to you.

Why do we develop unhealthy views?

The ending of a close relationship can be one of the most painful events in our lives. It's normal we should feel upset and distressed by this shake up. In fact, in this era of serial relationships, marriages and divorces, many more people are experiencing serial traumatic break-ups like this than in previous generations when people tended to choose their spouse young and stay permanently hitched.

Who is more likely to choose Option A over Option B? There are many different reasons why people respond in particular ways to personal loss: childhood experiences, history of fractured relationships, current support systems. However, underlying our emotional distress are our dysfunctional beliefs. These unhealthy attitudes are reflected in critical phrases like 'I must' or 'others should'. Karen Horney, the renowned psychotherapist, coined the term 'tyranny of the shoulds'.

Men and women with Option B responses tend to set themselves and other people such rigidly high and unrealistic expectations that, when they don't meet these high goals or someone lets them down, they end up feeling excessively frustrated, disappointed or angry, and viewing themselves as incompetent or unworthy.

In the heartbreak example, some of the faulty reasoning fuelling the distress and pain is likely to be: 'I *must* be loved by this person. If not, it means there's something wrong with me.' Or, 'All my other friends are getting married and settling down, I mustn't be the only one who's single.' Or, 'I should be married by the time I'm thirty because if I'm not I'll be left on the shelf.' Or, 'I should be in a relationship because if not I'll never meet anyone else and will end up all alone.' Or 'I must be in a relationship with someone I love because to be single is unbearable.'

Destructive interpretations and beliefs like these would turn even the most confirmed egomaniac into a quivering wreck, especially since these self-defeating conclusions are unlikely to be true. Let's look at the evidence. Where's the proof that someone is destined to be alone for the rest of their life simply because one relationship ends? Where's the proof that someone is unlovable, worthless or unattractive because another person fails to appreciate his or her charms? There is none.

Another problem with this train of unhelpful, unhealthy thinking is that such people tend to adopt an all-or-nothing stance. If we deem something good, such as having a relationship, we see it as absolutely, one hundred percent brilliant. Likewise, if we perceive something as bad, like being single, it's one hundred percent dreadful, awful beyond belief. However, in reality, very few things are either totally fantastic or completely terrible.

Most things in our life fall somewhere in the middle. So, even if your dream is to get married and have children, I'm sure you can muster up at least a few positive reasons why the single life's not so bad until you hook up with Mr or Ms Right. You can come and go as you please. You don't have to worry about a partner not liking certain friends. You can wear what you want. You can let your cat sleep on the bed. You can live where you want, paint the rooms the colours you want, and buy the furniture you want. You've got freedom.

BUILDING A MORE BALANCED VIEW OF LIFE: THE INFLUENCE OF THE BIG FIVE ON EVERYDAY PROBLEMS

We've had the theory. Now we're going for the practice. Time for you to learn the skills of CBT, so you can begin using them in your own life.

Throughout the book, I've been referring to five key factors – social situations, physical sensations, behaviours, emotions and thoughts – and the ways they interconnect and affect our lives. These big five determine if a **social situation** is stressful, fun, boring or awkward, and signal to our brain to produce corresponding **physical sensations**. Laughter when we're happy. Shakiness when we're anxious. Blushing when we're embarrassed. Tears when we're sad. Our **emotions** are also governed by our thoughts. We grieve at the sad thought we've lost a loved one. Our heart sings with joy when we fall in love. Our chest swells with pride when we've achieved a major milestone. Last, but not least, our **behaviours**. We clench our fists in anger. We shrink away when rejected. We smile when we're happy.

I've briefly alluded to this combination of mind-body factors before and detailed some of the ways they interconnect. Now it's time to look at their influence in more depth.

Our environments and thoughts

Let's start with our surroundings. There's no doubt that our environment shapes how we think, both in the long-term and the short-term. In the field of psychology there's been a debate raging for decades about the relative influence of nature versus nurture on our personality, mental well-being and thought processes. Although the jury's still out, it's pretty safe to conclude that our beliefs, behaviours and emotions are formed to some extent by both powerful forces.

I only need to turn to my clinical caseload for examples of this. Many of my patients and clients have had severely traumatic childhood experiences. Penny is one such person. She's addicted to heroin, crack and tranquillisers, and in addition to her substance misuse, was referred to me for help with her emergent memories of sexual abuse during childhood, which were so traumatic they were causing her nightmares and leading to increased drug abuse.

Penny was the eldest of nine children. Her mother had supported herself and her family through prostitution and Penny, like all her siblings, was conceived as a result of these 'professional' liaisons. Penny's early home life was rife with neglect – her mother drank and used drugs excessively – violence and brutality. Either my client was knocked about by her drunken mother or sexually abused by her 'patrons'.

From a very young age, Penny took it upon herself to care for her mother and protect her younger siblings. She never left the flat for fear of leaving her brothers and sisters alone or of her mother abandoning them and running off with a 'boyfriend'.

Needless to say, Penny missed out on her own education and friendships as she did her best to shield her younger brothers and sisters from the harshness of their existence. Keeping her promise to safeguard her siblings, Penny stayed in that violent hellhole until her youngest brother grew up and moved out.

Sadly, her own life was far from trouble-free after escaping. With no education or skills, she turned to petty theft and shoplifting to survive. Despite witnessing her mother's addictions, she also turned to drugs to block out the pain of her childhood and the bleakness of her present circumstances. Without a solid, stable background in which family members treated each other with love, concern and respect to fall back on, Penny turned to any man who'd take her in. The beatings and the black eyes were a small price to pay, in her mind, for a roof over her head and the occasional cuddle. When she did find a decent man, a loving partner, she became pregnant, had a child and dreamed of happiness for the first time. Sadly, domestic bliss was not to last. Her boyfriend, the one truly kind person in her life, died one day of a heart attack. He was thirty-five. Penny was shattered. Her drug use escalated and her son was taken into care due to her neglect.

A timid, fearful, anxious woman when I first met her, Penny had understandably reached the bleak conclusion that the world was threatening, dangerous cruel and abusive. With such a background who could blame her for holding these views?

Fortunately, most of us didn't have to endure the childhood horrors of Penny's upbringing, but our backgrounds don't have to be as traumatic to influence the way we think about and view the world. The generation in which we were raised, our culture, societal mores, gender, sexual orientation, class, parents, religion, teachers, peers and the media, also play their role in shaping how we think and feel about ourselves and the world.

Take society's current pervasive obsession with female body shape and excessive thinness. Talk about irrational beliefs and faulty reasoning! So unrelenting is this desire for extreme slimness that the upper end of the healthy, normal womanly weight range is considered fat, slovenly and ugly.

Personally and professionally, I can't think of many more damaging constraints on present-day women than this all-pervading attitude that a female's worth is dependent almost exclusively on her dress size. Women today have more personal freedoms, more academic and career choices and opportunities than our grandmothers even dreamt possible. And do females bask in these? Do they hell. So powerful is the 'thin is everything' culture that even liberated women imprison themselves in the endless pursuit of diets and weight-loss fads.

It shouldn't even have to be said, but women are worth more than their vital statistics. I am ashamed of this female obsession, especially since our predecessors struggled so hard for the right to vote, to hold on to their property, to educate their minds, for equality inside marriage, for equal pay. The battle's still not won entirely. Surely we've got more important ways to spend our time than in counting calories?

Of course, negative cultural pressures aren't just confined to women. Men often complain they have to contend with the pervasive expectation of their being 'masculine', or more precisely 'macho', which is often equated with emotional austerity, hardness, athletic prowess and success. These pressures are equally damaging. Go to any hospital accident and emergency room on a Saturday night and what do you find? Men who've drunk themselves into oblivion and started fights to prove how tough and strong they are.

As a clinician I often see how closely tied a man's sense of self-worth is to a strong-man identity – whether it's in the boardroom or on the football field. This morning, I met Dominic for our weekly therapy session. He embodies many of these culturally imposed masculine pressures. He's a keen football supporter of the violent hooligan variety. He drinks excessively, and goes around with a gang of his friends beating up the supporters of opposing teams. He's always gained a huge sense of self-importance from being hard, tough and strong. Until about a month ago, that is. At one such football match, on one such occasion, Dominic was struck from behind on the head with a baseball bat. Although he was lucky in that he didn't sustain any serious physical injury, his self-esteem took a huge knock. You see, in being attacked suddenly from behind, Dominic realised he wasn't all-powerful, all-invincible, and this was made worse because all his friends witnessed the event. As a result, his sense of masculinity and self-esteem suffered substantially. He'd lost face in front of his violent friends and so resorted to unhealthy drinking, drugs, and other self-injurious behaviours to cope with his newfound insecurities.

I live in hope that one day our self-esteem as individuals will no longer be dictated by such petty, superficial and harmful expectations dictating how we should think, feel and behave. My point is, however, that once attitudes and beliefs are formed, they tend to become deeply engrained, beyond our conscious awareness, and as a result are powerful forces which shape our lives.

Our physiology and thoughts

When we find ourselves in situations that affect us, either positively or negatively, our bodies respond in kind. Look back to a stressful occasion. Maybe it was the first day of your final exams. Or when you were sitting at a restaurant table wondering when or indeed if your blind date, now thirty minutes late, was ever going to show up. Or when you were walking up the steps to the home of your potential in-laws for the first time. No doubt your stomach was clenched tightly, your legs were a little on the weak side and feeling like they were about to give way underneath you, your heart was thumping a little too wildly in your chest and your voice was sounding squeaky and weak.

Think now about a happy event. The birth of your first child, your graduation ceremony or walking over the threshold of a new home. You were probably bursting with excitement, teeming with energy, barely able to sit still you were so full of ideas, plans and positive hopes for the future. Your thoughts dictated your physiological state.

A common problem that CBT therapists treat is anxiety. Because its physical symptoms are so severe and can be disabling, this disorder is a useful way of further illustrating how our thoughts affect the way we feel physically.

Many people rely on their morning cup of coffee (or two or three) to rouse them from sleep and propel them into action for the day ahead. What we sometimes forget, however, is that caffeine is a powerful stimulant and we can feel its effects on our system for several hours. Even after just two or three cups of strong coffee, people often complain of feeling shaky and light-headed, their heart racing. Sometimes people can mistake these symptoms for a heart attack. They convince themselves they're going to die and start to panic. Increased anxiety, in turn, exacerbates the accelerated heart rate, leading to a greater conviction of cardiopathy and imminent arrest. The end result is often a full-blown panic attack resulting from an excess of stimulants and the power of the mind.

Our emotions and thoughts

Learning to identify, understand and evaluate feelings is central to the CBT process. Let's say you've been asked to give a presentation in front of colleagues at work. As you stand up and talk, your boss fails to look at you. In fact, he begins to yawn and eventually you look over and notice that he's closed his eyes and is snoozing. What thoughts enter your mind at this point? Maybe that your boss is bored by what you have to say? How does that make you feel? Most likely sad, dispirited, worried and incompetent.

Since our thoughts govern our emotions, and because our perspective on our personal situation tends to be subjective not objective, we can often end up upsetting ourselves unnecessarily. Here's another possible explanation for this scenario: your boss had a late night and only caught a few hours' sleep. How would you feel if you knew that? Annoyed? Relieved? Indifferent? Surely not insulted?

The trouble is once a thought occurs to us it can be doggedly persistent. We scour around looking for evidence, both past and present, to support our initial beliefs and appraisals. Furthermore, when we're sensitive, or in a heightened state of emotional arousal as my scientific colleagues would say, it only increases the likelihood of our focusing on the negative and ignoring other possible explanations. Furthermore, we extrapolate based on this faulty logic. To extend the previous scenario: 'My boss finds me boring, so much so he can't even stay awake during this twenty-minute presentation. I know he doesn't like my work, he criticised the last report I gave. Maybe I'm just not up to the job? Maybe my colleagues think this way too? I'm probably just humiliating myself, making a fool out of myself. Why do I even bother?'

Is this an emotional hair shirt or what? All this self-loathing and negativity on the basis of a single fleeting impression. Again, just because something's thought, doesn't make it fact. Of course, I'm not saying our thinking is always faulty whenever we're feeling upset, down or distressed. The trouble is, however, whenever we have these overriding emotions we tend to overlook the balanced view. For example, when someone is having difficulties finding a job, he or she probably dwells on all those times he or she was unsuccessful and forgets about the times they were successful in landing a job. Most people think like this. The important thing is first to recognise these as distorted views, because understanding and identifying irrational thinking is the first step to healthier, more balanced, constructive thoughts and emotions.

Our behaviour and thoughts

In addition to influencing our emotions, our thoughts also affect the way we behave. We're just not always aware of it because many of our reactions and actions are automatic and have developed over the course of our lives. It's not so much a case of acting without thinking, as acting with subconscious thinking.

In my daily practice, I had one client who illustrates this point perfectly. Carol was a fifty-year-old high-powered lawyer who lacked assertiveness in dealing with her overpowering mother. Although this woman was a veritable Rottweiler in the courtroom, she was, in sharp contrast, a mouse at home who submitted meekly to her domineering mother's every demand.

Nothing Carol did ever met her mother's approval. She was constantly criticised for her choice of clothing, her friends, husband, housekeeping practices and child-rearing. Carol could do nothing right and was frequently undermined by her mother to such an extent that she even doubted her abilities to run her home. Privacy was out of the question. Her mother demanded to see Carol's phone bills, bank statements, even her personal diary! It's an interesting irony, this, that my client, a seemingly fierce legal eagle, was treated like a recalcitrant, irresponsible adolescent.

Why would Carol put up with such humiliation? After meeting my client for an introductory session the answer became obvious. Irrational thoughts were to blame. You see, even though Carol was a grown-up woman in her fifties, she was still her mother's child. Certain powerful and persistent thoughts, such as 'I must do what Mother wants because otherwise she'll be upset';

'good daughters should honour their parents, not talk back to them'; 'my mother will yell at me if I stand up to her' came to the fore. These were the cognitive culprits underlying all Carol's frustration and self-demeaning behaviour.

After a further session or two, she could now see that, as a grown woman, she was entitled to make decisions about her own life without having to feel bad about disagreeing with her mother or establishing firm boundaries. After all, an essential requirement of parenthood is to prepare children for their eventual independence. Furthermore, Carol was also able to understand that she'd behaved in this submissive manner to her mother all her life, she just hadn't been aware of it. Once I pointed out these irrational thoughts and analysed their appropriateness and validity, my client was halfway to making positive changes in her life. Mainly, developing a healthy, happy, autonomous relationship with her mother and understanding that independence was not synonymous with disrespect.

Carol's not unique. All of us have behaviour patterns that are automatic, knee-jerk reactions triggered by our environment. Because they are largely hidden from conscious view, we repeat them over and over as we've learned to do. It's only when we're forced to pay attention to them that we can analyse and evaluate them, and tease out the underlying thoughts that govern them.

How about your life? How do you react to your surroundings? Maybe you're someone who always puts everyone else's needs before your own, or tries to keep the peace during heated discussions and arguments, or rolls up your sleeves and mucks straight in whenever a crisis arises. Most of the time our behaviours are appropriate. However, from time to time, we find we wish we'd reacted differently during an awkward moment or stressful event. As in Carol's case, learning to identify the faulty thinking lurking behind the behaviours is an important step towards positive change.

EXERCISE 26:
IDENTIFYING THE BIG FIVE

Understanding the influence of the big five is easy. Learning to disentangle and differentiate between them is less so. In fact, it can be very difficult to distinguish one from another, particularly in the beginning stages, but it's essential that you do so because this is the heart of CBT. The following exercise has been designed with this goal in mind. Look at each item and decide which category (emotion, thought, behaviour, situation or physical feeling) it falls into. To get you started, the first three have already been done for you.

1. Angry (emotion)
2. At work (situation)
3. Shouted at my partner (behaviour)
4. Stomach upset
5. Meeting a friend for coffee
6. Thrilled
7. Waiting at the airport
8. Thumping heart
9. Bad things always happen to me
10. Visiting the in-laws
11. Waiting to be called in for a job interview
12. Seething
13. Light-headed
14. My boss is never happy with my work
15. Saturday morning
16. Excited
17. I hope my presentation goes smoothly
18. Loving
19. Waiting for a blind date to arrive
20. Arguing with my mother
21. Driving the children to football practice

22. Headache
23. Sweaty palms
24. Why do people always take advantage of me?
25. Joyful
26. Dry mouth
27. I'll never get that promotion
28. Resentful
29. My parents always preferred my siblings
30. Insomnia
31. Avoiding a friend following a row
32. Going for a run
33. Society is obsessed with youth
34. Boredom
35. Smoking
36. Blushing with embarrassment
37. Irritability
38. Slamming down the phone
39. Giving partner the silent treatment
40. Tingly fingers

And the answers are:

1. Angry (emotion)
2. At work (situation)
3. Shouted at my partner (behaviour)
4. Stomach upset (physical feeling)
5. Meeting a friend for coffee (situation)
6. Thrilled (emotion)
7. Waiting at the airport (situation)
8. Thumping heart (physical feeling)
9. Bad things always happen to me (thought)
10. Visiting the in-laws (situation)
11. Waiting to be called in for a job interview (situation)

12. Seething (emotion)
13. Light-headed (physical feeling)
14. My boss is never happy with my work (thought)
15. Saturday morning (situation)
16. Excited (emotion)
17. I hope my presentation goes smoothly (thought)
18. Loving (emotion)
19. Waiting for a blind date to arrive (situation)
20. Arguing with my mother (situation)
21. Driving the children to football practice (situation)
22. Headache (physical feeling)
23. Sweaty palms (physical feeling)
24. Why do people always take advantage of me? (thought)
25. Joyful (emotion)
26. Dry mouth (physical feeling)
27. I'll never get that promotion (thought)
28. Resentful (emotion)
29. My parents always preferred my siblings (thought)
30. Insomnia (physical feeling)
31. Avoiding a friend following a row (behaviour)
32. Going for a run (behaviour)
33. Society is obsessed with youth (thought)
34. Boredom (emotion)
35. Smoking (behaviour)
36. Blushing with embarrassment (behaviour)
37. Irritability (emotion)
38. Slamming down the phone (behaviour)
39. Giving partner the silent treatment (behaviour)
40. Tingly fingers (physical feeling)

How did you do? If you got five or more answers wrong, you might want to review the previous section and take the quiz again before you move on.

EXERCISE 27:
STARTING CBT

Since the big five are all linked and influence each other, it follows logically that small changes in one of these areas will also affect the others. But, before change is possible in your life, it stands to reason that you first need to identify these factors in the first place. This process, however, isn't easy for the uninitiated CBTer. In time and with practice it will become like second nature for you to identify these five facets, to develop the skills to overcome your problems and to transform your life.

Practice is the key to perfecting these techniques. Because the steps involved are complex, I thought you might find some examples from my clinical and corporate caseloads helpful as templates for you to follow.

Work scenarios

The secret to CBT's success is its flexibility and applicability to just about any situation we find ourselves in. And some of the more stressful situations I know of stem from the workplace. Do any of these scenarios ring true with you?

First, let's look at the challenges Jack currently faces. He was fifty when he first came to see me. He'd been referred by his doctor to help him boost his confidence and self-esteem.

When I met Jack everything about him – his posture, lack of eye contact, slow gait, flatness of voice – screamed low self-esteem. Over the past six months or so, he'd complained of a number of worrying symptoms that were plaguing him: sleepless nights, loss of libido, lack of appetite, persistent feelings of deep despair. He no longer seemed to enjoy his favourite hobbies or going out with his friends. Usually a happy-go-lucky sort of man, Jack had become irritable and short-tempered; so much so, he'd snap at his wife and children over trivial things.

On the surface, Jack seemed to be suffering from the classic symptoms of depression. When a biological cause for his low mood had been ruled out by his physician, he and I looked at some of the psychological factors which might be underlying his distress. It didn't take us long to find the answer. Six months ago, Jack lost his job as a senior sales rep for a major company when the organisation decided to downsize. Jack loved his job and was very successful. So, although he was understandably unhappy about his recent change in work status, Jack wasn't unduly concerned about securing another position. Unfortunately his optimism was misplaced. Despite sending in CV after CV and being invited in for a few interviews, Jack remained unemployed.

Derek was another client. He'd been referred to me initially for anxiety management. A young man of thirty-four, Derek had been working for the same insurance company since leaving college twelve years before. A hard-working and dedicated employee, he loved his job and threw himself into the company culture. He organised the yearly Christmas bash and was a star player for the organisation's football team. Needless to say, his commitment and loyalty paid off. He rose quickly through the ranks to a senior executive position, the youngest ever vice-president. He and his young wife were financially secure and looking forward to starting a family fairly soon.

Everything was sailing along smoothly in terms of his career until one fateful Thursday morning when suddenly he could no longer face his job. On that day Derek was driving to work as usual. However, the closer his car got to his office building, the more he began to feel anxious and panicky. So much so that instead of turning into the car park, Derek just kept going and spent the entire day driving around. The next morning he summoned up the courage to try again. But nothing doing. The nearer he came to his office building, the more his symptoms of anxiety accelerated.

Terrified he was having a nervous breakdown, Derek drove straight home. During the past months, he's barely left the house.

Then there's Melissa, a twenty-eight year old working for an advertising agency. She'd always set her sights on this field and, after graduating from college, took the first job that was offered her, a secretarial position. Since this glamorous field was highly desirable and jobs in it hard to come by, however lowly, Melissa was grateful just to get her foot in the door. Full of ambition, she worked hard and, like Derek, was rewarded for her efforts. She soon became an assistant account executive, then was quickly promoted to account executive and finally senior account executive.

The other day, Melissa's boss called her into her office. They were opening a new branch of the agency in Sydney and the powers that be wanted to send Melissa Down Under to help set up the new office. Another promotion, prestigious job title and boost in salary were all part of the deal, but Melissa would need to make a two-year commitment to the position.

Flattered and excited about the opportunity of working in Australia, in her dream job to boot, Melissa felt she was walking on air. It was all too good to be true. Suddenly euphoria turned to fear. With this opportunity came added responsibility. Was she qualified and competent enough to handle it? And what about the work colleagues here she adored, not to mention her family and boyfriend? How could she leave them? What if her romantic relationship couldn't survive the distance? Besides, she didn't know anyone in Sydney. What if she didn't like it there? What if she couldn't make any friends? On the other hand, dream offers like this don't come around every day. How would it look professionally if she turned it down?

Swinging between excitement and self-doubt, Melissa couldn't make up her mind. She knew she'd have to give her boss a decision fairly quickly. In the meantime, Melissa was doing her best to avoid her.

Relationships

Of course, our problems aren't limited to the workplace. If only. Difficulties are just as likely to arise in our personal relationships with partners, parents, children, in-laws and friends.

Meet Alison. She's a forty-four-year-old divorced mother of two teenage children. Alison was married for almost twenty years, but despite her divorce has a good relationship with her ex-husband. She also enjoys close ties with her children and her parents.

What's the problem then? With her children growing up and almost ready to leave home, Alison has recently met someone special, a potential partner even, and would like to embark on this exciting new relationship. But she's concerned that her ex-husband, children and parents won't approve because the new love of her life is female.

For as long as Alison can remember, she's always been sexually attracted to women. Despite her lesbianism, she went out with and eventually married James and later gave birth to a son and a daughter. For a number of years, she was content with her life as housewife and mother, even though her physical attraction to other women didn't completely fade away. However, as the years passed, Alison's relationship with James became rocky and they eventually decided to separate. Nothing dramatic happened, they just drifted apart.

Having met Paula recently at her local gym and spent a little time with her, Alison can no longer ignore their mutual attraction. However, even though she'd like to be open about her sexuality and her feelings for Paula, Alison is fearful of 'coming out' to her family and friends because she's afraid of disapproval and rejection. So much so, she's developed headaches and eczema through stress.

Then there's Edward. He is thirty-one, happily married to Jessica for three years now. She's intelligent, beautiful, generous and great fun. Edward, besotted by this lovely creature, couldn't believe his luck when she agreed to be his wife.

Not everything is blissful, however. The trouble is, Jessica and his mother can't stand each other. In fact, they loathed each other on first sight. Every Christmas, family wedding or Sunday lunch since has been strained and fraught with tension for Edward. His wife and mother always find fault with one another, bicker and become incensed at some imaginary slight. He loves them both, loves spending time with each. He just hates spending time with them together.

Not only does he become upset, anticipating the inevitable rows, he also feels powerless to do anything to improve relations between them. He's tried talking to them. He's tried sending them away to a health spa in the vain hope they'd get along once they got to know each other better. He's even tried to serve as an objective moderator as each aired their respective complaints. Nothing worked. What's worse is that each tries to persuade him to take her side, but of course he can't. One's his wife, the other's his mother. They're both important to him. Poor Edward. He really does feel like piggy-in-the-middle.

Problems between mothers- and daughters-in-law are as old as the hills, but what if someone's relationship problems involve people they haven't even met yet or don't know particularly well? Angela, a thirty-five-year-old single woman fits this bill. She is a bright, attractive, outgoing professional who's also one hundred pounds overweight.

Since all her friends are settling down and getting married, Angela too would like to meet the man of her dreams. In addition to her weight being hazardous to her health, Angela feels she'd be more attractive to the opposite sex if she shed some pounds. The trouble is, however, Angela can't stick to a healthy eating regime for very long. She's tried every fad diet in the book and might lose a couple of pounds, but before long she's back where she started. She resumes her old eating habits, snacking excessively, particularly when she's anxious or worried.

And nowhere is Angela more anxious or worried than when she's out on the town with her dwindling number of single friends looking for a prospective boyfriend. It becomes worse when she spots someone she's attracted to in a bar or nightclub. So much so, she can't summon up the courage to speak to them or even smile to make herself seem more approachable. Overcome by nerves, Angela keeps *schtum*, dances and chats with her friends, and goes home alone. Angry and annoyed with herself for her own cowardice, she turns to food for comfort in the privacy of her bedroom. Her weight increases and her self-esteem spirals downward.

And what about people who've met the love of their life only to find out there's a conflict in goals with their relationship? Take Laura's example. She is thirty-nine and has been involved with Richard for the past five years. In just about every way they get along really well. They are physically attracted to one another, share the same sense of humour, enjoy outdoor sports and like each other's families. In just about every way Laura feels they're perfect together. However, the fly in the relationship ointment here is Richard's profound antipathy to marriage and children. Laura's biological clock is ticking; she's tried talking to Richard, explaining her very real concerns about potential childlessness. She's tried prying out of her partner a guestimate of just exactly when he might want to settle down. She's threatened him with an ultimatum: marry me within a year or it's over. But Richard is resolute. Even at the age of forty-two, he feels he's much too young to settle down and doubts if he even wants children at all.

Laura still loves Richard, can't imagine a life without him. The problem is, she can't imagine life without being a mother either. She's in a real dilemma and this is badly affecting her mood.

Social events where young children and babies are present make her tearful, and hearing of friends' pregnancies is very painful.

These are all real people, with real problems. Their pain was real too. All feeling trapped in their situations, fearing they'd never find a resolution to their problems. CBT, however, helped them all.

The first step I took in each case was to help my client analyse their difficulties by breaking them down between the big five. I asked them to take some paper and a pen and write down: situation, physical sensations, mood, thoughts and behaviour, so that they could begin seeing how these factors interact with and influence each other.

Very shortly, I'm going to ask you to look at your own personal stresses and strains in a similar way. However, to give you some practice, I now want you to do the following exercise. Using each of my client-case scenarios, I'd like you to break down their problems according to situation, physical sensations, thoughts, emotions and behaviours. The answers need only be very brief. One or two should be enough. So, have a go.

1. What's going on in Jack's environment? What are his feelings likely to be as a result? His behaviours? Physical symptoms? Thoughts?

2. What situation is causing Derek distress? What are his physical feelings? His emotions? His perceptions? How did he respond?

3. What about Melissa? What are the recent changes in her life causing her uncertainty? How have they impacted on her mood? The way she behaves? Her physical health? Her thoughts?

4. Then there's Alison. What is she feeling about her situation? What are her perceptions? Her emotions? Thoughts?

5. What's happening in Edward's life that's posing him difficulties? Can you describe his feelings? What about the physical symptoms? His behaviour? His thoughts?

6. Let's not forget Angela. What problems is she facing? How do they affect the way she feels emotionally? Physically? How does she behave as a result? What conclusions does she draw?

7. And finally, Laura. What's her situation like? Can you describe her emotions? What about her physical feelings? How would you describe her behaviour? And her thoughts?

The point of this task is to help you learn to disentangle these different factors and strands. So, with your shrink's pad in hand, doctor, how did your analysis go? This is how the patients and I worked together.

1. **Jack**

    Situation: loss of job
    Physical feelings: sleeplessness, loss of libido, appetite problems
    Emotions: depression
    Thoughts: I'll never get another job
    Behaviours: withdrawing from friends, snapping at family, not looking for work

2. **Derek**

    Situation: Driving to work
    Physical feelings: anxiety
    Emotions: fear

Thoughts: I must be having a nervous breakdown, I'm letting my wife down
Behaviours: driving around, not leaving his home

3. **Melissa**

    Situation: promotion opportunity overseas
    Physical feelings: sleeplessness
    Emotions: fear, uncertainty, unhappiness
    Thoughts: I don't know if I can do this new job, what if I can't make friends?
    Behaviours: avoiding boss

4. **Alison**

    Situation: new relationship
    Physical feelings: stomach pains
    Emotions: fear of rejection
    Thoughts: I want my family to love me, I want to have a relationship with Paula
    Behaviours: conceals gay relationship from family

5. **Edward**

    Situation: family gatherings attended by wife and mother
    Physical feelings: stress
    Emotions: distress, frustration, powerlessness
    Thoughts: Why can't we all just get along for once like other families? I hate being forced to take sides. Why can't I come up with a solution?
    Behaviours: persisting with joint family occasions

6. **Angela**

   Situation: meeting potential boyfriends
   Physical feelings: butterflies in her stomach
   Emotions: self-consciousness, fears of rejection,
   disappointment, loneliness
   Thoughts: They won't like me anyway, so what's the point
   of approaching them?
   Behaviours: comfort eating

7. **Laura**

   Situation: when she goes to weddings or her friends
   announce they're pregnant
   Physical feelings: sleepless nights, worry
   Emotions: sadness, envy, fear
   Thoughts: I either have to stay with Richard and never have
   children or go out and try to meet someone else
   Behaviours: Looking on the internet for potential new
   partners

Breaking our problems down like this helps give us a clearer picture of the difficulties we're going through and our reactions to them. It also paves the way for feasible, viable solutions.

It's not the final step, it's just the beginning. The key to exploring healthier, more helpful responses is analysing our thoughts. In many ways, we humans are all natural psychologists. We look at our lives, our friends, our boss, and can't help analysing situations and trying to make sense of things that happen to us. Often we get it right; on other occasions we get it wrong. Even when we're one hundred percent convinced we see our situation clearly, people are prone to what psychologists call 'attribution errors' or misjudgments. It's that old emotional reasoning that gets in the way every time.

It is clear, therefore, that the way we look at and assess our problems has a huge impact on the ways we cope with them. When I presented their analysis to each of my clients, it became the first step towards evaluating a coping strategy.

Jack, for instance, when questioned further realised he attributed his current unemployed status solely to the belief that others saw him as past his best and, as he couldn't turn back time, in his mind there was no hope on the job front. Since he loved sales work and enjoyed the status it had conferred on him, Jack was understandably devastated when the company he worked for went out of business. His subsequent lack of success on the job front only reinforced his sense of loss.

At first, Derek couldn't quite put his finger on the reason for his anxiety and for his avoiding work. It was only after a few sessions together that he came to see the true source of his difficulties. All his life he'd been the 'responsible one'. When he was a child, his father died and his mother came to rely on him as the new 'man of the house'. He did quite a lot of the cooking when she was at work and looked after his younger brothers and sisters: helping them with their homework, disciplining them, teaching them to drive.

What's more, he always put everyone else's needs before his own. That's what was expected of him; that's what he did. However, at the age of thirty-four, after achieving career success and with the prospect of starting a family on the horizon, he understandably felt burnt out. Somewhere in the back of his mind Derek was terrified that he was going to grow old before his time, before he'd even had a chance to be young. His anxiety was borne out of an inner conflict between his duty to his wife and career, and the desire to be a young man and have some fun.

With Melissa, this exercise helped clarify some of her thoughts and fears about breaking free from what was familiar and safe and venturing out into the scary unknown. Melissa had always been a homebody. She was the only child of parents who married well into their forties. They never thought they'd be able to have children, so when Melissa came along, she was much cherished, adored and doted on. They were such a close family unit that when she was beginning to think about moving away from home to attend a large university several hundred miles away, she detected such sadness in her parents' eyes she couldn't bear the thought of their loneliness without her. So she opted for a degree course closer to home. She lived at home throughout and only moved out a year ago, but still lives within an hour's drive of her family home. Melissa lives with two former school friends and she's known her boyfriend, Steve, since childhood.

Melissa loved her job in advertising. It was her dream job and she really thrived in it. She wanted more than anything to continue her steep rise to the top, but hadn't realised these opportunities would lead her to Sydney – about as far away as she could possibly get from her family, friends and Steve. It was only natural she'd be nervous, but she had a choice to make. Fear could either paralyse her or, if addressed, lead her to grow, not just professionally but personally.

Our relationships, like our careers, also pose dilemmas for us. Let's look at Alison's seemingly no-win situation. I can appreciate it's not always easy, even in this day and age, for people to be open about their homosexuality to their nearest and dearest. In fact, it's often more difficult to render ourselves vulnerable and share such secrets with our family and friends.

Alison felt trapped and indecisive. She really wanted a relationship with Paula but was terrified her mother would disapprove, maybe disown her. She was also worried about how her children would react to having a lesbian mother. Alison was concerned too about losing Paula.

We explored a little background: I asked about Alison's family and their attitudes towards homosexuality. She laughed. Her family never discussed sexuality, either hetero or homo. She loved her parents, but it was a fairly distant relationship. Her mother and now deceased father never discussed any personal or intimate details of their lives. Family gatherings or conversations were usually limited to general news about children, trips to the vet, holidays, the latest film. Alison also reported that her parents were very conservative, if not prudish, about sex. For as long as her brothers and sisters could remember, her mother and father had had separate bedrooms and they'd learned from childhood that discussions about sex were strictly verboten. So, homosexuality was definitely off limits as a topic.

As for her children, Alison was concerned they'd reject her and Paula. Or, even if they did approve of their mother's new relationship, might be leaving themselves open to ridicule at school. How could she ever cope with that kind of guilt?

Paula understood Alison's situation but her patience was starting to run thin. This was the twenty-first century, for God's sake! Besides, Alison's children would be leaving home themselves in a few years. Did she really want to risk missing out and ending up alone?

Relationships are difficult at the best of times. Throw in divorce, children, conservative parents and homosexuality, and they become a recipe for even greater tensions.

Even when people are open about their relationships, conflict can be unavoidable. Look at Edward's situation. He's so stressed out about his wife and his mother, he barely knows which way to turn. This exercise helped him understand his feelings about the relentless arguments. I asked him about his family background and he said he was an only child. His mother was always a strong-willed character who ruled the roost, while his father, deceased for five years, was more mild-mannered and gentle. He never raised his voice and was happy to let his wife make all the decisions. Edward, who was similar in temperament to his dad, was also attracted to feisty, fiery women. It was no surprise to me that wife and mother, with their outspoken natures, clashed. Because he was unaccustomed to speaking his mind and more used to playing the role of peace-keeper, the value of this task was chiefly to allow Edward to talk about his emotions, his sense of powerlessness and desire for peace, his sense of responsibility towards his mother now that she was widowed and the strain it placed on him.

And what of Angela? From the moment she burst into my office, I found her bright, bubbly and lots of fun. I'm no Weight Nazi and, as I've written earlier, feel we set too much store on women's appearance. However, I was concerned that Angela's weight was both physically and psychologically damaging to her. From a physical perspective, I was worried that severe obesity could lead to problems with her health. We also needed to talk about the emotional side of her excessive eating. By completing this exercise, Angela was able to see that her relationship with food had replaced any relationship with a man. What's more, food was always reliable, safe, would never criticise or reject her, and was available any time she wanted. In many ways, the ideal partner.

And, finally, we have Laura. Many women can relate to her predicament. After kissing more than her fair share of frogs, she finally found her life's companion, Richard. But despite their loving relationship, these two had reached a seemingly insuperable stalemate. She wanted marriage; he didn't. She wanted children; he didn't.

Unfortunately, though women have achieved equality (well, sort of) in many areas of their lives, when it comes to reproduction our biology is very much the same as our prehistoric grand-mothers'. Richard, of course, had the option of procreating well into his dotage, but Laura did not have time on her side. She knew that life without him would be unbearably difficult. Equally, she understood she'd only resent him come the first symptoms of menopause.

EXERCISE 28:
USING CBT IN YOUR OWN LIFE

Now it's your turn to look at situations and circumstances you've experienced or endured that have caused you to feel unhappy, defeated, stressed or fed up. Grab your notebook and answer the following questions.

Situational triggers

Have you experienced any changes in your life recently? What have been the most stressful situations in your life for the past year? Past three years? Past five years? Childhood?

Physical reactions

Do you experience any troubling physical symptoms in response to difficult situations? Decrease in energy? Stomach aches? Headaches? Dizziness? Loss of interest in sex? Sleep disturbances? Vague aches and pains? Breathing difficulties? Chest pains? Muscle aches or heavy limbs? Concentration lapses?

Emotions

How would you describe your moods in response to upsetting situations? Sad, nervous, afraid, guilty, ashamed, embarrassed, anxious, envious, overwhelmed?

Behaviours

Has your behaviour changed as a result of these situations? Did you become more reticent? Withdrawn? Were you more likely to shout? Lose your temper? Engage in unhealthy or reckless behaviours such as drinking, taking drugs, spending excessively? Crying?

Thoughts

When you experience a stressful situation, what kinds of thoughts go through your head? About yourself? Other people? Your future? Your past? What images and memories come to mind?

When we are unhappy, upset, unfulfilled or feel dissatisfied with our lot in life, there is a tendency to bury our head in the sand in the hope that all the nasty stuff will disappear by itself. Although this course of action is tempting – after all, it's not easy to address our personal difficulties, in fact, it can be downright painful or unpleasant – if difficulties are not addressed head on, they usually persist and it requires more and more effort to block our unhappiness from our minds. As a result, to make ourselves feel better, or distract our thoughts from our worries, we often engage in behaviour that's less than beneficial. We even give coy therapeutic names to some of these activities. Drowning our sorrows. Retail therapy. Comfort eating. But we know the truth, of course. We can drink vats and vats of *vino*. Punish the plastic from dawn till dusk. Eat ourselves into oblivion. And, yes, they really do make us feel better. But only in the short-term. After an evening or a day, not only don't our problems fade away, but we're hungover, in debt and struggling to fit into our clothes.

This may seem very obvious, but we can't change our behaviour until we're consciously aware of how we react, and sometimes the point needs to be hammered in a few times.

Making the conscious links might be fairly straightforward; changing behaviour less so. We are creatures of habit, even those that are harmful or prevent us from achieving our goals. This is because familiarity allows us to creep safely within our comfort zones. New skills, even beneficial ones, are scary. When the therapeutic mirror is placed in front of our faces, we might not always like what we see in the reflection. We might not be quite as good or as brave or as secure as we like to tell ourselves. But, while recognising our behaviour is a vital step to change, so is venturing out of the comfort zone.

Step One: Choosing a situation to work on

The notes you just made were meant as a taster so you could start analysing your life the CBT way. Perhaps you're having difficulties at work? Maybe it's your boss, your colleagues or the simple fact that your job's simply not challenging enough for you? Perhaps a family member is being particularly antagonistic? Maybe you find you've got an important decision hanging over your head and don't know which way to proceed?

Let's see how we can work to resolve your dilemma. Choose one stressful situation and write it down.

Even if you find the overall situation or circumstance particularly distressing or difficult to cope with, say a bullying boss, it's always helpful for the CBT process to be specific about the situation you want to analyse. The more specific you are, the more likely you are to tap into precisely those negative feelings and faulty pieces of logic that are causing you unhappiness.

So, instead of writing down 'my bullying boss', which is too general, I'd like you to record a particular incident in which your boss bullied you. For example: 'On Friday morning, at our weekly team meeting, I mentioned I'd heard about a creativity and problem-solving training session and thought it might be really useful to generate new ideas. My boss rolled his eyes and sighed.'

Step Two: Corresponding physical reactions

Next, I'd like you to chart any physical reactions you noticed as a result of this stressful moment. One- or two-word answers will do here. If we take the above example, we might record: thumping heart, shaky hands, tight stomach, sweaty palms.

Step Three: Corresponding behaviours

The next step in the process is to record how you responded. Again, you can keep the words and phrases simple. 'I blushed because I was humiliated, apologised for my silly suggestion and kept quiet for the remainder of the meeting.'

Step Four: Corresponding emotions

The next two categories we need to consider are our corresponding feelings and thoughts. They're generally not quite as straight-forward as the others and sometimes require a bit more work.

Let's take our feelings first. Identifying unpleasant feelings, even when highly motivated to do so, is not always a straightforward task. It usually takes quite a bit of practice to tease out emotions from thoughts, memories and impressions, because they're so intertwined and usually deeply buried. To complicate matters even further, when we're upset or experience a strong emotion, such as anger or sadness, it's a pretty sure bet that there are other emotions lurking about. Furthermore, because the feelings triggered by unpleasant or upsetting moments are usually, understandably, pretty unpalatable, many people prefer to block them out entirely.

If you want to refresh your memory on the way we experience and express emotions, you might want to spend a little time going over the information in week one. As a brief reminder, let's take an example. When a relationship ends, many people claim sadness is the overwhelming emotion they feel. If they scratched the surface, they might also recognise anger, resentment, loneliness, fear and abandonment. If the job we've been angling for goes to our best friend at work, sure, we feel happy for them, but disappointment, jealousy, rejection, maybe a little guilt for our lack of loyalty and support, are also likely to creep in.

Since we have to identify the whole range of our feelings

before we take steps to change them, I want you to think about a situation, in the past or recent present, which triggered a noticeable emotional response in you. Since negative emotions might be a bit too threatening to start with, begin with the positive. Think about an event or circumstance which left you with a pleasant feeling. Maybe it was a wedding, a promotion, quality time with your family? The specific occasion doesn't matter as long as you were left feeling well within yourself.

Now, I want you to scroll down the following list of words and identify all the positive emotions that reflect that situation.

Happy
Ecstatic
Excited
Proud
Cheerful
Loving
Calm
Content
Confident
Surprised
Loved
Connected
Close
Competent
Accomplished
Flattered
Generous
Caring
Energised
Motivated
Grateful
Hopeful

There are no right or wrong answers here. The purpose of this exercise is merely self-exploration and to get you into the practice of identifying all the various emotions and feelings we usually experience. No doubt you've been able to identify at least a handful of pleasant feelings associated with this positive event, even if at first only one predominant emotion came to mind. You might have even identified one or two negative feelings – guilt for taking time off from work or embarrassment for having so much attention bestowed upon you. That's normal. Even our greatest highpoints and achievements sometimes come at a little cost, just as long as we don't allow them to ruin our day.

Now take a closer look at the negative feelings. If you have particular personal difficulties you're not yet ready to face up to, that's okay. You can always choose a situation that made you mildly upset. Once you've envisioned this event in your mind, write it down. Next, look at the list below and identify all the unpleasant feelings associated with this situation.

Sad
Ashamed
Anxious
Angry
Frustrated
Enraged
Bored
Disappointed
Disgusted
Betrayed
Guilty
Scared
Hurt
Embarrassed
Nervous

Intimidated

Belittled

Insecure

Apathetic

Impatient

Lethargic

Rejected

Hopeless

Helpless

Impotent

Incompetent

Insignificant

Resentful

Annoyed

Jealous

Dealing with negative emotions is obviously a less pleasant experience than identifying positive ones; we don't always necessarily want to be reminded of these occasions or of our behaviours and reactions as a result.

If you're okay with the situation itself, but still can't quite put your finger on all the different negative emotions stirred inside you, try this. Scan down the list. How did you feel after each word? Did you feel tense? Tightness in the stomach perhaps? A little anxious? If so, then there's a good chance the corresponding emotion resonates within you. Which was the predominant feeling? Did others emerge that weren't in this list? Analysing skills only develop with practice and dedication, so keep at it, you'll get there in the end.

Let's look at some of the clients I introduced earlier and their experiences of this exercise. When I first met Jack, he already felt his confidence had been knocked but was surprised to find there was underlying anxiety and a sense of hopelessness about his job situation. Derek hadn't realised that he was also suffering from guilt, boredom and anger. Melissa was surprised that feelings of insecurity and fear had emerged. In Alison's case, it was guilt. With Edward, Angela and Laura previously unrecognised symptoms of anger, resentment and powerlessness emerged. All were surprised by their discoveries, but in teasing out all or several of their suppressed emotions, each one agreed the realisation made a lot of sense.

Now, getting back to the corresponding emotions part of the exercise, I'd like you to think about the stressful situation you identified. First, I'd like you to write down as many emotions as you can think of triggered by this event. Three to five will do. Then, I'd like you to rate the severity of these emotions on a scale of 1 (least severe) to 10 (most severe). Here's an example from my bullying boss scenario: I felt embarrassed (9), humiliated (9), nervous (7), incompetent (7) and alone (8).

Step Five: Corresponding thoughts

Pivotal to the CBT process are our thoughts, beliefs and attitudes. In order to work on developing healthy, happy beliefs, we first need to learn to identify them. This is not as easy or as straightforward as it might sound. Thought-spotting is a skill that takes some practice. Think about when you first learned to drive a car. Maybe one of your parents showed you how or perhaps you went to a driving school for special instruction. When you think back to the moment you sat behind the wheel for the first time, you were probably a little nervous, wondering how you were going to remember everything. Three-point turns, parallel parking, driving in dangerous weather conditions, tackling busy roads. It was all a bit daunting in the beginning – so much so you might have even wondered how you'd be able to keep your mind on the road ahead – and you probably had to concentrate hard to fine-tune and perfect this new skill.

After a while, however, as you became more and more adept at driving, you probably found you no longer had to concentrate so intently on the actual mechanics of the car. And, before long, the skills were now so practised they became automatic. To the point where if you actually forced yourself to itemise the sequence of putting on your seatbelt, turning the key in the ignition, checking for ongoing traffic, etc, the process would be cumbersome. The procedure is the same for thought-identification.

THOUGHTS RECAP

Thoughts fuel the emotions we feel

Thoughts also underlie our behavioural patterns and influence the actions we choose to take or not to take

Our attitudes, beliefs and perceptions are usually formed during childhood and carry on throughout adulthood

Our perceptions are almost always subconscious, automatic processes

Becoming aware of your automatic thoughts

The following exercises are designed to help tap into your automatic thought processes. We human beings are constantly in the process of thinking, remembering, imagining and envisioning, even if we're not actually aware of it. Throughout the day, thoughts, impressions and opinions pop in and out of our brains. Our minds are a veritable stream of cognitive processes. We daydream about the upcoming party we've been invited to, fret about a job interview next week, mentally itemise all the errands we need to get done. While all these might be examples of automatic thoughts, the type we're interested in here is those that govern our strong emotions.

As you go through each exercise, pay careful attention to strong emotional and physical reactions as you read. If you respond with sharp pangs in your stomach and your heart is racing, it's a good bet that the automatic thoughts are striking a chord with you.

EXERCISE 29:
AUTOMATIC THOUGHTS QUESTIONNAIRE

The first exercise is a questionnaire which contains a large number of the more common automatic thoughts that people have revealed. The list is not exhaustive, it's indicative. So, in the process, if you find other subconscious beliefs pop to the fore of your mind, please write them down.

Listed below are a variety of thoughts. Please read each one and indicate how frequently, if at all, it occurred to you over the last week. Please read each item carefully and circle the appropriate answer on the sheet below in the following fashion (1='not at all', 2='sometimes', 3='moderately often', 4='often' and 5='all the time'.

Then, please indicate how strongly, if at all, you tend to believe that thought when it occurs. On the right-hand side of the page, circle the appropriate answers in the following fashion (1='not at all', 2='somewhat', 3='moderately', 4='very much', 5='totally'.

Frequency	Items	Degree of Belief
☐	1. I feel like I'm up against the world.	☐
☐	2. I'm no good.	☐
☐	3. Why can't I ever succeed?	☐
☐	4. No one understands me.	☐
☐	5. I've let people down.	☐
☐	6. I don't think I can go on.	☐
☐	7. I wish I were a better person.	☐
☐	8. I'm so weak.	☐
☐	9. My life's not going the way I want it to.	☐
☐	10. I'm so disappointed in myself.	☐
☐	11. Nothing feels good anymore.	☐
☐	12. I can't stand my situation.	☐
☐	13. I can't get started.	☐
☐	14. What's wrong with me?	☐
☐	15. I wish I were elsewhere.	☐
☐	16. I can't get my life together.	☐
☐	17. I don't like myself.	☐
☐	18. I'm worthless.	☐
☐	19. I wish I could disappear.	☐
☐	20. What's the matter with me?	☐

☐ 21. I'm a loser. ☐

☐ 22. My life is a mess. ☐

☐ 23. I'm a failure. ☐

☐ 24. I'll never succeed. ☐

☐ 25. I feel so helpless. ☐

☐ 26. Something has to change. ☐

☐ 27. There must be something wrong with me. ☐

☐ 28. My future is bleak. ☐

☐ 29. It's just not worth it. ☐

☐ 30. I can't finish anything. ☐

(Adapted from Hollon and Kendall (1980), 'Cognitive self-statements in depression: Development of an automatic thoughts questionnaire', *Cognitive Therapy and Research*, 1980, 4, 383–95. And *Mindfulness-Based Cognitive Therapy for Depression: a new approach to preventing relapse*, Zindel, Williams and Teasdale (Guilford Press, 2002).)

EXERCISE 30:
THOUGHT SCENARIOS

Read the following scenarios and write down any automatic thoughts that come to you.

Scenario One

You're at the supermarket, stocking up on your weekly supply of food. As you turn down one of the aisles, you happen to notice one of your friends talking to a mutual acquaintance. They look up in your direction, you wave, but they don't respond. Instead, they carry on the conversation and begin walking away from you. What are your automatic thoughts?

Scenario Two

Your birthday's in a week's time and it's a big one. You're feeling far from festive. In fact, the last thing you want to do is celebrate being another year older. You tell your family and friends that you just want the day to pass like any other. Unnoticed. Unmarked. No cakes that are potential fire hazards because of the number of candles required. And, on the big day, that's exactly what happens. No one wishes you a happy birthday. No cards. No 'for s/he's a jolly good fellow'. What are your automatic thoughts?

Scenario Three

After years of working in one particular job, you decide you've had enough and go about the long, arduous process of changing careers. After a master's degree in your new field, in addition to your previous management experience, you land a job in a good company. Your new boss is a few years younger than you. Although she's got more experience working in this particular work environment, you're more educationally qualified and have years more management experience.

On your first day of work, she calls you in to welcome you. She tells you she's impressed with your resume and is made a little insecure by your achievements. She even jokes about having to watch you in case you try to steal her job. What are your automatic thoughts?

Scenario Four

You've always wanted to see the world. After years of spending your holidays with your oldest friends at their beach cottage, you feel it's time to go farther afield. You've always wanted to go to Thailand, and you've decided that this is definitely the year to go. You inform your friends that they'll be holidaying alone this year because you're off to Bangkok. Instead of wishing you *bon voyage*, as you expected, they start fretting about the dangers of travelling to the Far East. What are your automatic thoughts?

Scenario Five

After years of working in a job that no longer inspires you, you decide it's high time for a career change. Since you've always wanted to work in broadcasting, you start exploring opportunities at local stations. After months of trying without any luck, a station manager offers you some work experience. In exchange for this, you act as the gofer. Not great, but why not?

The more you think about it, the more excited you become. You go home and tell your family and your friends. However, one of your friends also has news for you. Your quest for this exciting new career has prompted her to change jobs, too. Guess what? Without any broadcasting experience at all, she lands a job at the very same station where you're expected to work for free. Opportunities like this always seem to fall into her lap. What are your automatic thoughts?

Underlying automatic thoughts

These five scenarios are pretty common, in one shape or another. However, our automatic, underlying thoughts are likely to be unique to ourselves and not shared by others. In the first scenario, some people might have been tempted to respond 'I always knew they didn't like me', 'They're talking about me, I can tell', or 'I bet they find me so boring, they didn't even want to stop and say hello'. In other words, they interpret the situation as a negative appraisal

of themselves. In contrast, others might have read the scenario
along these lines: 'They looked so engrossed in their conversation,
I bet they didn't even see me. I'll call them later and say hello.' Or
possibly, 'I can't believe how rude some people can be.'

In scenario two, what kinds of beliefs did you find emerging
about the birthday? Some people are quite happy to let the
anniversary of their arrival in this world pass without any fuss and
would therefore be pleased their wishes were heeded. 'I'm glad the
day was low-key because I've always hated being the centre of
attention on these occasions. I know my family was disappointed
because they really wanted to do at least something, but I'm pleased
they honoured my wishes.' By contrast, others might have felt a few
twinges of hurt when the day arrived, despite their earlier
insistence. 'How could my family and friends completely ignore
the day? I know I said I didn't want a fuss, but surely if they loved
me they would have insisted on some form of celebration?'

It's always very exciting to start a new job, in an exciting new
field, whatever age we are when we decide to take the plunge. And,
of course, there are a number of advantages older people offer the
workforce. Maturity, experience, confidence . . . to name just a few
valuable skills. That said, the workplace is rife with insecurities,
conflict and competition. In scenario three, what automatic
thoughts sprang to mind? 'I'm flattered that someone in my
exciting new career values my abilities and skills'? Or how about, 'I
worked hard to redirect my career and I'm pleased my efforts have
been rewarded. However, I shall have to make sure my boss doesn't
feel threatened by me. I want her to view me as an asset to the
team'? Or, finally, 'I've worked really hard to change careers
because the atmosphere in my last job was so competitive and
hostile. I thought I'd left all that behind. Maybe I made a mistake?
Maybe I should look for another job?'

And scenario four? You're all excited about your trip to
foreign fields. You've never even travelled out of the country before

and so venturing to exotic Thailand is such a thrill. What thoughts emerged when your friends failed to share your sense of adventure? Did you think along the lines of 'Maybe they're right. I've never been abroad before and know nothing of Thailand. I'm not ready for this. Better cancel my ticket'? Perhaps instead you came to this conclusion. 'I know it's a big step going so far from home, but I'll be careful and not do anything risky. Besides, danger can arise anywhere.' Or maybe you thought, 'We've been going to their beach house for ten years. They'll feel lonely if we don't come this summer. I think we should spend some time with them before we go.'

And, finally, the fifth scenario. An old friend lands the job you've been telling absolutely everyone within earshot you're dying to get. What thoughts spring to mind? 'How dare she apply for a job I wanted? She wasn't even interested in broadcasting until I began mentioning it'? Or maybe instead your thoughts fall along these lines. 'She always gets everything she wants. It's so unfair.' Or perhaps, 'It's great to have a friend working there. She could be useful in supporting my application when another job arrives.'

Exploring automatic thoughts

Of course, there are lots of plausible subjective reactions to each of these scenarios. Don't be surprised or disappointed if yours differed from mine. It's also feasible to hold a number of automatic thoughts at the same time, even ones that seem contradictory.

Now that you're more practised in this technique, I want you to think back to the stressful or unpleasant situation you previously identified and the corresponding physical sensations, behaviours and emotions. Once you've done that, I want you to think about and write down the underlying, automatic thoughts triggered by your adverse circumstance. Between one and three is what you should aim for here.

If you remember the example I used earlier, involving the young woman with the bullying boss, her corresponding automatic beliefs would probably look like these:

1. My boss really hates me. Every time I see him, he scowls at me.

2. I can't believe I made that suggestion about the training seminar. Everyone thought it was a stupid idea. They probably think *I'm* stupid now.

3. I get so nervous whenever my boss is present, I start to stutter and blush and just come across as silly and incompetent.

4. My colleagues are so hostile and so unsupportive. I was hoping one of them at least would have stood up for me.

5. They must really think I'm incompetent. I bet I'll lose my job. Then what will I do? I obviously won't get a good reference, and I'll probably end up working for a fast-food chain.

If you're still having problems teasing out your underlying thoughts, maybe you're trying too hard. Here's a suggestion. Close your eyes and imagine you're back in your own stressful moment. How did you feel physically? How did you behave? What was your mood like?

Now answer each one of the following questions:

1. What was going on in your mind directly before you started feeling negative emotions?
2. If these thoughts are true, what do they say about me and my abilities?
3. What do these thoughts reveal about me and my future?

4. What am I worried about?
5. What is the worst-case scenario?
6. What are other people likely to think about me?
7. With these questions pointing you in the right direction, what are your automatic thoughts?

AUTOMATIC THOUGHTS RECAP

Thoughts, impressions, images, memories, daydreams and opinions pop into our heads spontaneously throughout the day.

Whenever we have strong feelings and emotions, there are usually automatic and subconscious thoughts underpinning these reactions.

To identify underlying cognitions, it is often helpful to focus on what's going through your mind whenever you have a noticeable emotional reaction.

Week Eight:
Developing Healthy Beliefs

Welcome to the penultimate week of the program. Last week's instalment should have helped you to understand the ways in which environment triggers off a whole chain of reactions. The way we learn to overcome our problems is through first identifying all the different facets and strands that contribute to them.

This week, the theme is developing effective coping mechanisms for overcoming and resolving problems, enabling you to be in control instead of being controlled. You'll feel competent and able, because you *will* be competent and able. Such is the power of CBT. Once you get the hang of it, it's so simple.

For now, I just want you to take a few moments, close your eyes and imagine how it would feel to be the kind of person who could handle anything. Feels pretty good, doesn't it? That person will be you by the end of this program.

But we're getting a little ahead of ourselves here. Before we proceed further, as ever, I want you to continue incorporating the following tasks and exercises into your week's plans:

1. Looking after your health
2. Thirty minutes of physical exercise at least three times per week

3. Ten to fifteen minutes' relaxation every day
4. Improving sleep
5. Mirror exercise
6. Random acts of smiling
7. Exchanging good news
8. Thirty minutes a week on your hobby
9. Blue dot exercise
10. Keep up with daily task list
11. Take time to reflect

How about another anecdote to warm you up and get you in the CBT mood?

It is a dark and stormy night. A man is driving along a dark country lane, rushing to get home to his wife who's threatened to leave him. Suddenly, without warning, a thunderstorm breaks. The heavens open. So much so, that visibility, which was already difficult, now becomes extremely hazardous. With the rain pelting down and the driving conditions treacherous, the man can barely see anything through the misty windscreen and struggles hard to maintain control of the car. He'd pull over and wait for the conditions to subside, but he needs to get home tonight. He must press on, his wife has given him an ultimatum. Either he makes it home tonight to discuss their marriage or she's gone.

Suddenly, there's a clap of thunder and a lightning bolt strikes a tree up ahead. It falls across the lane. The man swerves to try and avoid it, to no avail. He loses control and smashes into the fallen tree. He gets out to inspect the damage and realises with dread that his car's going to have to be towed. He tries calling his road recovery service but can't get a signal on his phone. In sheer frustration he kicks the car hard and slips on the muddy road. Cursing himself and the heavens, which are drenching him further with every passing second, he frantically wracks his brain for some kind of escape route.

In a sudden burst of inspiration, he remembers a farmhouse a few miles back. This is his only solution. Despite the thunderstorm and the risk of drowning, he has no choice but to seek help from there.

As he sets off, he finds the route back a real struggle. The country lane has turned into a mud slide and he can barely maintain his balance as he plods steadily but slowly forward. He falls down a number of times, covering himself head-to-toe in mud, and sprains his ankle when he accidentally steps into a pothole.

The man is overwhelmed by fatigue. Only the thought of saving his marriage motivates him to keep limping on. An hour passes and he's only halfway there. The rain is still pouring down, the wind still howling. He's soaked to the skin and by now in physical agony, so much so he doesn't even know if he can keep going. And something within him has finally snapped. He curses the heavens, his own bad luck, he even begins cursing the people in the house ahead. He starts muttering to himself, like a man possessed.

'What a hell of a night! I've crashed my car, sprained my ankle, ruined my brand new suit. I'll never make it home tonight. My wife's probably already left me. There's no hope for my marriage now. And, after all this, when I do finally reach the house up ahead, I just bet the farmer won't even help me. He'll just stare at me and shake his head. Not letting me use his phone. Not calling for help on my behalf. Not offering me a cup of coffee. I'll be surprised if he even opens the door at all. He'll probably set his dogs on me or call the police. I can see it, I just see it. He'll stand there laughing at me, the jerk! Who does he think he is anyway? How dare he laugh at me?'

Fuelled by his anger, the man soldiers on and finally reaches the gate of the farmhouse. He stomps up the front path and bangs on the door. Before the farmer can open his mouth to speak, the man shouts at him and shakes his fist.

'Listen, you. You think this is funny, don't you? Well, I wouldn't accept your help now if you were the last person on earth, you selfish, cantankerous old man. The world would be a whole lot better off without miserable people like you in it.'

With these parting words, the protagonist of our tale turns around and storms off, through the rain and the mud, all the way back to his car, leaving the poor farmer deeply perplexed and wondering if a patient has escaped from the local mental hospital.

This pithy anecdote is not merely a humorous story, illustrating human foibles. Nor is it a cautionary tale of the horrors that will surely unfold should you let your automobile emergency recovery service subscription lapse. My intention here is to show how quickly and often unreasonably our thoughts and feelings spiral out of control.

In my work, I often find that clients become so wrapped up in their problems they can't disentangle them. They're too closely involved, simply can't be objective. However, if I asked my clients to comment on other people's problems, all of which are equally complicated, I suspect they'd quickly regain their perspective and even come up with viable solutions. This is no accident. You see, it's often much easier to give advice to someone else about their problems because we're detached from them. Our own emotions aren't invested in them. We don't get so worked up about them.

Let's pretend for a moment that you were asked to comment on the scenario above. What would you say to our wretched protagonist?

After giving him a towel and a cup of hot chocolate, you'd probably pick up on the fact that the pressure to race home to his disgruntled wife and the mishap of getting stuck in the storm had predisposed him to be foul-tempered, this whole unfortunate turn of events made even worse when he got drenched and sprained his ankle. You might mention that his thoughts had been spiralling out of control to such an extent that he assumed he'd receive a cold welcome from the farmer – a man he has in fact never even met before and has no prior knowledge of. What's more, his heightened emotional state, faulty logic and behaviour, fuelled though they were by frustration and pain, only made his predicament worse. Had the man been able to calm down and regain perspective, he would more likely have received the help he so desperately needed. He would probably have been given some food and maybe a change of clothes. Saved his dignity too. The outcome, in other words, would have been vastly different and to his advantage.

There's no doubt about it: sometimes, left to our own devices, we can be our own worst enemies. Luckily, however, using CBT techniques can help us maintain perspective and prevent situations getting out of control.

CHALLENGING EMOTIONAL REASONING

Becoming aware of the ways in which personally stressful situations can trigger a whole chain of adverse responses is the first step towards taking control of our lives. The next is to evaluate them so we can calmly and rationally plan how to respond.

It stands to reason that once you tap into your automatic thoughts, a variety of viable solutions will become available to you. You might find you've been spot on with your assessment of the situation, and the solutions will then probably seem fairly obvious to you. If, on the other hand, you decide your appraisal was not so reasonable or reliable, you can always work on revising your understanding of the situation. Not only will having a rethink buy you some time to regain a calm and collected frame of mind, but as you reassess you are less likely to behave in a rash way.

In CBT, we call this process 'thought challenging'. Once you master the art of challenging your own faulty emotional reasoning, you'll be able to handle any situation put in your path.

Validity checking

In CBT, healthy belief systems are synonymous with effective coping mechanisms. The more people are able to challenge their own emotional reasoning and replace these irrational, distorted beliefs with logical, reasonable ones, the more in charge they'll feel of their life. We start the process rolling by doing a validity check.

By this, I mean assessing the emotional reasoning. If we took our miserable, rain-drenched friend and asked him to itemise all the reasons why he was so convinced the farmer would ridicule him, slam the door in his face and generally be hostile, he might respond, 'No one ever cares about anyone but themselves, even when someone's in trouble.' This bleak sentiment is fairly common – that society's uncaring. It's every man and woman for themself. Since this is a conclusion he might well have drawn, it's perfectly understandable that his frustration would be exacerbated and his mood become more desperate.

However, if we step back a little and look more analytically at this negative if common view, I'm sure we can all agree that even if society is fifty percent unfeeling and hostile, even eighty or ninety percent, not *everyone* is so heartless. In fact, if this man were real, he'd probably be able to identify one or two or even several people who'd provided assistance to him in the past. On this occasion, because his frustrations were magnified by his automatic thought that no one would help him, he behaved in such an aggressive, frightening manner that even if the farmer had been predisposed to offer help, he would probably have feared for his own safety and moderated his response accordingly. And even if the farmer was a crusty, heartless curmudgeon, by behaving reasonably and calmly, the man might have persuaded him to make a phone call on his behalf or at least advise him where else he could find assistance. Instead, given the scenario, the farmer would far more likely call the police.

Step One: Identifying the big five

If you've completed the exercises from last week, then you've already identified at least one or two thought distortions and corresponding feelings and behaviours triggered by a stressful event. I'd like you to write down all five thought distortions on a piece of paper. Don't forget to rate the severity of your emotions using a ten-point scale (1=least severe and 10=most severe).

Since the CBT analytic process can be complex, I thought it might be helpful if I included my clients' scenarios as a template for you. Since validity checking is complex, it's always helpful to see the process in action, especially when the coping skill is largely unfamiliar and new. Furthermore, each of my clients has such varied problems, it's useful to see the sheer number and diversity of irrational thoughts we humans are capable of.

1. **Jack**

   Situation: Tuesday morning, 10 a.m. I overheard my wife talking on the phone. Her thirty-eight-year-old nephew, Ben, has just been made partner in his accounting firm.

   Physical feelings: I could feel my stomach clench and my heart start to race.

   Emotions: I felt jealous (7) because he had a job and I didn't, afraid (9) that I'd never be able to work again, powerless (8) to change my situation, angry (6) that my wife could be so happy for her nephew when her husband's out of work, and useless (9) now that I could no longer support my own family.

   Thought distortions: Only young men like my nephew get work these days. I don't stand a chance of ever getting any. I'm no use at all to my family if I'm not the breadwinner.

Behaviours: Stormed out of the room. Snapped at my wife for the rest of the day.

2. **Derek**

Situation: Thursday afternoon, waiting for my boss to arrive. He wants to speak with me about returning to work next month.

Physical feelings: Jittery, like I can't sit still, and anxious. The more I think of it, the more panicky I become.

Emotions: Fear (10), guilt (9) and self-loathing (9).

Thought distortions: I must be crazy. Why else wouldn't I be able to go to work? I'll never be able to work again. I'm letting my wife down.

Behaviours: Asked my wife to call and cancel the boss's visit and sat in my bedroom all day, refusing to talk to anyone.

3. **Melissa**

Situation: Monday afternoon at work, I received a message from the Sydney office. They wanted me to call them back urgently about the job.

Physical feelings: Massive adrenaline rush, light-headed, dizzy, nausea.

Emotions: I felt frustrated (8) with myself for not being able to make a decision. I felt pressurised (10) being put on the spot like this, and anxious (8) because I knew they were waiting for an immediate decision.

Thought distortions: I'll never be able to cope so far away on my own.

Behaviours: Left work early to avoid further phone calls from Sydney and spent the afternoon comfort shopping.

4. **Alison**

   Situation: Wednesday evening, phone call from my mother. The son of one of her work colleagues just got divorced and my mother wants to fix me up with him. I said no, but she's really pushing for me to go out with him. She said I've been alone too long and it would please her if I found a new mate. That I'd also be doing her a favour because she likes her work colleague a lot.

   Physical feelings: Tension headache, restless night.

   Emotions: Guilt (9), stress (8), fear (8), loneliness (6).

   Thought distortions: My mother would never approve of my lifestyle. Knowing that she'd never approve, I must be a deceitful daughter. She'd disown me if she knew I was a lesbian.

   Behaviours: I stormed around snapping at my children.

5. **Edward**

   Situation: Yet another family occasion, my cousin's engagement party last Sunday. My mother complimented my cousin on her 'excellent taste' in a spouse and said her fiancé would be a welcome addition to the family. My wife took these comments as a personal slight. By this time, she'd had too much champagne and started to make snide remarks about my mother. The other guests overheard and their antics ruined the festive atmosphere of the party.

   Physical feelings: Throbbing head and tingling limbs.

Emotions: Extremely angry (9), stressed (8), powerless (8), disappointed (7).

Thought distortions: Other families manage to get on well with each other. I wish my wife and mother would behave like normal people. I must help these two women like each other for the sake of the family.

Behaviours: I drove home in silence as my wife continued her diatribe against my mother. Once there, I locked myself away in my study and worked on my computer.

6. **Angela**

Situation: Saturday night. Dinner party at my friend Michelle's house. An old friend, Jake, was visiting and she thought we'd really hit it off. I bought a new dress, got my hair cut, really made an effort. I was so excited about meeting Jake. We sat next to each other at dinner, but he blanked me out. I tried making conversation with him, but he just wasn't interested in anything I had to say. He couldn't take his eyes off our other friend, Jessica. Thin, fit, beautiful Jessica. I might as well have been invisible.

Physical feelings: At first I felt excited because I was really looking forward to the evening. I couldn't sleep the night before, couldn't eat a thing. But as I sat there, just being ignored by Jake, how can I describe it? It's like my heart sank in my chest.

Emotions: Disappointment (9), rejection (9), self-loathing (8), loneliness (8), hopelessness(9).

Thought distortions: Everyone I know is paired off. What does it say about me that I'm alone? I'll always be alone. All my friends are settling down and getting married. I will only be happy if I get married too. I can't handle any more rejections like this one tonight with Jake. It's true what they say: beauty is only skin deep, but ugliness goes all the way.

Behaviours: I made my excuse to Michelle and left her party early. I was so upset. On the way home I picked up a pizza and some Cookies and Cream ice cream. I scoffed the lot. I felt better at first, then I started to feel guilty. I know I shouldn't rely on food to make me feel better, but I can't help myself.

7. **Laura**

Situation: Saturday morning. My old college's newsletter arrives and I find out an old friend has just given birth to her fourth child.

Physical feelings: My eyes welled up with tears.

Emotions: Sadness (9), jealousy (10), resentment (9).

Thought distortions: Life would be too sad and lonely without the prospect of children to contemplate. What kind of woman am I without children? Defective, pathetic, that's what. I'm not only a failure as a woman, I'm a disappointment to my parents. I know how badly they want grandchildren. I must be unlovable. If Richard really loved me he'd want to marry me and have children.

Behaviours: I couldn't stop crying and cancelled dinner plans with Richard and his friends. When he came home that night, I started shouting at him about leaving a huge mess in the bathroom and said that I was sick of picking up after him. He shouted back and stormed out.

Step Two: Looking for supporting evidence

Once you've had a chance to read through these different case scenarios, I'd like you to chart your own big five connected to your chosen incident in this style.

Next, I want you to look at the automatic thoughts that sprang from your particular stressful situation and write down all the evidence you can think of to support your conclusions. Some people in the beginning mistake their 'interpretation' of a situation for 'fact', so it's important you remain objective. 'I could tell by the look on her face that my wife no longer cares for me' is an example of interpretation. 'My wife scowled at me' is objective evidence.

Here are some examples using my clients' case studies.

Jack: He was understandably shocked and upset to be laid off from a job he loved. His hurt was magnified and his self-esteem took a further blow with every rejection and each passing month of unemployment. Jack's whole identity revolved around being head of the family, breadwinner and successful salesman. He began to believe he was 'half a man' without a job and was terrified he'd lost his prime, authoritative position in the family. His belief that he was too old to get another job only fuelled his negative perceptions of himself and the hopelessness of his situation.

When I asked him to come up with proof to support his thought distortions, he had no trouble.

1. Only young men, like my nephew, get work these days.

Society is obsessed with youth. Some of my colleagues have even resorted to cosmetic surgery, and I'm talking about the men, just to increase their chances of getting a job.

2. I don't stand a chance of ever getting work.

Every time I go on interview, they've hired someone younger even though they've had far less experience than me.

3. I'm no use at all to my family if I'm not the breadwinner.

I asked my son the other day, if he'd like me to come with him to pick out his new car, but he turned me down. That's the third time this month he declined my offer of help. My wife is always nagging at me to help around the house and do demeaning chores.

Derek: With some people, one or two automatic thoughts are particularly disabling. In CBT, we call such beliefs **hot thoughts**. These hot thoughts are the automatic thoughts a person has in reaction to a certain situation, and tend to focus on symptoms of the underlying problem rather than the problem itself. Derek is a case in point. Understandably he was concerned about his terrifying symptoms of panic and anxiety, and even though he knew in the back of his mind that he wasn't ready to settle down yet and start a family, that he wanted to have some fun and adventure, his hot thoughts focused on two themes: concerns about his own mental health and about letting his wife down.

When I asked him to identify all the evidence in support of his automatic thoughts, here's what he came up with.

1. I must be crazy. Why else wouldn't I be able to go to work?

Normal, mental healthy people are able to go to work without having a breakdown. There are hundreds of men and women who fit that bill in my office.

2. I'll never be able to work again.

All day I sit here and do nothing. Just the thought of returning to that job makes me break out in a panic attack.

3. I'm letting my wife down.

I must be a failure as a husband because I'm not providing for my family.

Melissa: She had always lived a very safe, sheltered life. Although she was a competent professional and loved her PR job, it seemed to me the true source of her anxiety about moving to Sydney stemmed mainly from her fears of branching out alone for the first time and living thousands of miles away from her parents, her boyfriend and her friends. In her mind, she was equating independence solely with loneliness. As she had never been on her own, she feared she wouldn't be able to cope.

I'll never be able to cope so far away on my own.

My parents have always been just around the corner, whenever I've needed them. If I took this job in Sydney, they'd be so far away.

I only spent a few days away from them in the past when I was fourteen and went to summer camp. I was so homesick I cried every day. They had to come and get me.

I've never been without my friends and family around me. I panic if I have to spend an evening by myself.

Alison: When Alison and I met to talk about her dilemma and first examined her automatic thoughts, it became clear that at the heart of her anxieties was her family's reaction to her sexuality.

Although she was physically attracted to Paula and liked her a lot, any potential relationship would be a dead duck without her family's support and approval. It's not that she meant to hurt Paula or lead her on, but Alison was coming to the conclusion she'd want to come clean with her family and deal with any possible fall-out before even thinking of falling in love.

The telephone call from her mother about the blind date had thrown Alison in a spin. It was crunch time. She couldn't really avoid the issue much longer, hence her anxiety. What if her mother rejected her completely?

1. My mother would never approve of my lifestyle.

She didn't speak to me for three weeks when she found out I was getting a divorce, because she said it was wrong for me and my husband to part.

2. Knowing that she'd never approve, I must be a deceitful daughter.

Most daughters I know of try to please their parents, and here I am involved in something I know my mother wouldn't approve of.

3. She'd disown me if she knew I was a lesbian.

My mother is very religious. The Catholic Church frowns on homosexuality. I really upset her with my divorce. I don't think she'd tolerate another major shock.

Edward: He had been pulled in two opposing directions, by his wife and mother, from the moment he got engaged. With every family occasion a veritable battleground, Edward felt forced to choose sides. He loved both women, had loyalties and responsibilities to both. How could he choose? When we investigated his thoughts and feelings a bit further and looked at the evidence he came up with in support of his automatic beliefs, it became clear that Edward tended to look to other families as a gold standard of behaviour.

1. Other families manage to get on well with each other. I wish my wife and mother would behave like normal people.

I've never noticed any conflicts or arguments or quarrels whenever I've gone to visit friends or colleagues. They always seem to enjoy each other's company.

2. I must help these two women like each other for the sake of the family.

If I don't help these women get along, who will? There's no one else who can sort their situation out.

Angela: When Angela came to see me, there was no doubt in my mind that her self-esteem had taken quite a beating. As she sat in front of me, crying over her lack of a boyfriend, it was clear she needed to build her self-confidence, independent of her dating desires, and break this cycle of binge-eating.

1. I'll always be alone.

All the desirable women in the world are a size 6. Just look at the fashion magazines and the Hollywood actresses.

Fat people are the subject of ridicule. We're seen as lazy and unhealthy.

2. All my friends are settling down and getting married. I will only be happy if I get married too.

Every time I go to bars and night clubs, I see hordes of single women looking so desperate and sad. Television programmes and movies always portray single people as bitter rejects.

3. It's true what they say: beauty is only skin deep, but ugliness goes all the way.

I haven't had a date in years now. Every time I approach men in night clubs and bars, they pretend they don't see me.

Laura: Her painful dilemma was obviously breaking her heart and a lot of issues were brought to the fore through this exercise. She knew that sooner or later she'd have to make a choice. Either stay with Richard, a man she'd loved for several years, and probably never have children, or leave him and hope she'd meet another man with his qualities who was ready to settle down and have children.

Furthermore, Laura's pain was heightened because she saw it as her duty as a woman and daughter to produce children. In her mind she wouldn't be a 'real' woman if she never experienced childbirth and child-rearing.

She also saw Richard's hesitation to settle down and marry as a reflection on her own worth.

1. Life would be too sad and lonely without the prospect of children to contemplate.

The happiest women I see have children. Women who've never had them always come across as sad, as if they couldn't find someone to love them.

2. What kind of woman am I without children? Defective, pathetic, that's what. I'm not only a failure as a woman, I'm a disappointment to my parents.

My parents wouldn't dream of saying anything to me, but I can tell by the way they play with my sister's baby that they want more grandchildren.

I read in the newspaper the other day an article about this woman banker. She killed herself when she found out she couldn't have any children. That she'd left it too late.

3. I must be unlovable. If Richard really loved me he'd want to marry me and have children.

My sister told me that I was wasting my time with him. She said he wasn't against marriage, he was against marriage to me but too lazy to go out and find a new relationship. Richard knows me better than anyone. If he doesn't love me, I must be unlovable. I never had much luck with relationships in the past. So, maybe he is staying with me for convenience.

You: Now it's you turn to identify all the evidence you can think of in support of your automatic thoughts.

Step Three: Evidence disputing our automatic thoughts

Helping my clients articulate and write down all the reasons in support of their faulty thinking is essential if we want to assess their validity. They also help tease out any deeply embedded fears and lingering thoughts that needed to be voiced. If they're not brought out into the open, they can act as blocks and barriers.

Now, I want you to take another look at this evidence. Scan

through that of my clients. Peruse yours. What did you notice? Certainly in the case of my clients, quite a lot of their 'evidence' has a ring of plausibility about it. Jack is right. We do live in a highly ageist society, revere youth, disrespect the elderly. And what about Derek's concerns about being labelled mentally ill? The mentally ill are also victimised by society. Melissa was right too in some ways. Moving away from home to a foreign country is a daunting experience for even the most confident of people. And who could dispute Alison's viewpoint? Our parents' approval and affection is very important to us. Edward's desire for a 'normal' family was also not unreasonable. Most families don't spend all their time bickering and fighting or treating each other with open hostility. As for Angela, I couldn't dispute her point that society overvalues physical appearance. And, finally, we have Laura. She's also right in her views that children provide great joy for couples and, of course, grandparents.

The point about validity checking, however, is this. Our conclusions, even if they're seventy or eighty percent true, are unlikely to be one hundred percent true. And, even with a margin of twenty to thirty percent, there's still room to manoeuvre. There's still hope.

Let's look at the supporting evidence my clients wrote down as proof for their beliefs and examine it objectively. I asked them each to appraise their evidence and come up with counter-evidence.

Jack's Thought-challenging Evidence

1. Only young men, like my nephew, get work these days.

My twenty-three-year-old son and several of his friends had a rough time finding work when they first left college. Some of his friends are still looking.

2. I don't stand a chance of ever getting work.

Come to think of it, I went on one interview for a job and the position was given to a man two years older than me.

3. I'm no use at all to my family if I'm not the breadwinner.

That weekend my son didn't want me to go shopping with him because he and my wife were organising a surprise birthday party for me to cheer me up. I only found that out yesterday.

It's true that my son didn't need my help on those three other occasions when I offered, but he did ask me to look after my grandchild and to help him with his taxes.

My wife always tries to give me encouragement and support, even when I'm bad-tempered and snap at her. I know that she's tired from working all day and it's only reasonable for her to expect me to help out around the house.

Derek's Thought-challenging Evidence

1. I must be crazy. Why else wouldn't I be able to go to work?

I understand now that anxiety is a common affliction. My father used to have panic attacks from time to time and so did a work colleague. They both received treatment and are now living active, productive lives.

Besides, I was the one who recognised I had a problem and went to the doctor for help. Even though I was really scared that I was going bonkers, I was able to address my problems and seek solutions.

2. I'll never be able to work again.

My father and colleague eventually went back to work and so do millions of others. There's no reason why I shouldn't be able to go back to work too.

Besides, I've worked hard all my adult life and still have my skills. They haven't disappeared. Even in the time I've had off, I've learned computer programming and designed and built a garden shed.

3. I'm letting my wife down.

I might be going through a bad patch now, but I've always been a good husband to my wife. I've worked hard in a job I despise so I could provide her with a nice home, a car, trips abroad. I've always been faithful and devoted to her. Besides, if she were going through a crisis, I'd be there for her. For better or worse and all that.

Melissa's Thought-challenging Evidence

1. I'll never be able to cope so far away on my own.

My parents might be physically far away, but Sydney's not on a different planet. We could easily keep in touch by phone and e-mail. Australia's only a plane ride away. If things got too tough, I could be back home within a day.

I'm no longer fourteen, I'm a grown woman now. A mature, responsible career woman. The PR position in Sydney is a dream job come true, not a boring, miserable summer camp I never wanted to go to in the first place.

I hate being on my own, but I suppose I could make friends in Sydney the same way I did at home. Through work, the tennis club and business networking organisations.

Alison's Thought-challenging Evidence

1. My mother would never approve of my lifestyle.

It's true she was upset about my divorce, because she's a Catholic. But she wasn't angry for too long and really helped me out. She babysat my kids whenever I had to work late. She was always cooking dinner for us, because she knew I was tired after a long day at the office. She even offered to lend me money if ever I needed it. My mother turned out to be a big support.

2. Knowing that she'd never approve, I must be a deceitful daughter.

I don't intentionally mean to lie to my mother or hurt her. I'd never purposely do that. I'd like to be honest about my sexuality with her, but I need to find the appropriate opportunity first.

I didn't ask to be gay. I didn't go out of my way to upset her.

In many ways, I like to think I'm a devoted daughter to my mother, despite our differences in attitudes. I take her to her appointments with her doctor and hairdresser. I call her several times a week. I love my mother. She's very important to me.

3. She'd disown me if she knew I was a lesbian.

My mother's cousin is gay. Although she doesn't openly talk about it, she obviously knows he's homosexual and they've always been very close.

My relationship with Paula would run much deeper than sex. She's a great person and if my mother got to know her, I know she'd like her as much as I do.

My mother was upset about my divorce. I was brave enough to take the risk that she'd reject or disown me. At some future stage in my life I'm sure we'd disagree again or I'd have to make choices she wouldn't like. Mothers and daughters aren't always going to agree on the way they run their lives.

Several of my friends decided to 'come out' to their families. Their parents' attitudes were similar to my mother's. It was easier for some than others, that's for sure, but no one was disowned.

Edward's Thought-challenging Evidence

1. Other families manage to get on well with each other. I wish my wife and mother would behave like normal people.

I suppose since fifty percent of marriages now end in divorce, not all families get along well with each other all the time. Now that I've been asked to think about it, many families I know have their problems too. My boss was telling me the other day how he's dreading spending next weekend with his mother-in-law. Kept calling her a loathsome old battle-axe. My wife's best friend fell out with her family over a will. They haven't spoken in three years. My cousin's son was expelled from school for taking drugs. All things considered, I guess my family situation is fairly normal.

2. I must help these two women like each other for the sake of the family.

To be honest, I can't come up with any good reason why *I* must be the one to help them resolve their differences.

My family hasn't fallen apart simply because those two can't stand the sight of each other. They're both mature women who are more than adept at handling their own affairs. I've tried everything I can think of to resolve their differences; maybe I've done all I can.

It's their problem, not mine. Maybe they should decide for themselves if, when and how they will bury the hatchet.

There's no law that says every single family member has to love each other. Is there?

Angela's Thought-challenging Evidence

1. I'll always be alone.

Always is a long time. I've had relationships in the past. There's no feasible reason why I can't have at least one more at some point in the future.

Marilyn Monroe, another size 16, is still considered one of the sexiest women of all time. For all her fame, perfect body and beauty, Princess Diana was notoriously unhappy, particularly in relationships. Maybe thin people aren't always happy.

2. All my friends are settling down and getting married. I will only be happy if I get married too.

It's true that many of my friends have got married and settled down. However, some have also got divorced.

One of my friends, who got married at twenty-eight, feels she was far too young to settle down. A new friend at work is recently divorced. She has a full social life, splurges on herself, does what she wants, when she wants. She's the happiest person I know.

3. It's true what they say: Beauty is only skin deep, but ugliness goes all the way.

I've never met a decent date in a bar or club yet. A friend at work showed me a magazine article about a psychological study which found couples who met in bars were the least likely to stay together. Couples who met through friends or mutual interests were much happier. Maybe I should try to meet men through other means.

Just because some men don't find me attractive, doesn't mean *All* men don't. I got whistled at just the other day and an acquaintance told me I had a beautiful smile. My past boyfriends all liked me for who I was and none complained about my looks or my figure.

Laura's Thought-challenging Evidence

1. Life would be too sad and lonely without the prospect of children to contemplate.

Come to think of it, I work with several women who juggle career and child-rearing and they look exhausted most of the time. They say they love their children, but as soon as they became 'Mother', they lost their individual identity. They miss the freedom of being single and having time for themselves.

Some of my work colleagues have even said to me they envy my lifestyle. *My* lifestyle! One or two have even confided in me that their children are selfish and ungrateful. If they had to do it all over again, they'd think twice about sacrificing their lives to raising them.

My Aunt Ginny never had children and she travels all over the world. She's got friends on every continent and knows she's always got a home here with my mother and father should she ever get lonely or bored. She's an anthropologist and really loves her life. She's never lonely or bored.

A friend suggested I could always have my eggs frozen or adopt a child. I don't have to rely solely on Richard to provide me with children.

2. What kind of woman am I without children? Defective, pathetic, that's what. I'm not only a failure as a woman, I'm a disappointment to my parents.

I've met my Aunt Ginny's fellow anthropologists. Many don't have children and they don't see themselves as failures or second-rate women. They believe women should develop their minds and contribute to society.

My parents have never, ever told me they're disappointed in me for not providing them with more grandchildren. In fact, they've always said they're proud of me for going to Harvard and forging my career. My mother even said she's envious that I have opportunities she never even dreamed possible.

3. I must be unlovable. If Richard really loved me he'd want to marry me and have children.

Richard shows me in so many ways that he loves me. He took care of me when I was sick. He surprised me recently with a dream weekend in Bermuda. He stayed up all night helping me fix my computer because he knew I needed it for a business trip the following day.

Yes, I've had dating disasters before I met him, but these experiences aren't a reflection on my current relationship. If anything, they've shown me you've got to kiss a few frogs before you find your prince.

Even if Richard left me tomorrow, my parents and my friends love and care about me. Being lovable doesn't just depend on some man validating me as a woman.

You

Now it's your turn. Take another look at the automatic thoughts you identified and once again at the evidence you've written down in support of them. Next, I want you to challenge your distorted beliefs in the same way that my clients did. Just make sure that your counter-proof is credible and strikes a chord with you. If you spout some half-hearted facts that might loosely contradict your assumptions then the exercise will be a waste of time. So, no trite reflections such as 'The sun will come out tomorrow' unless you absolutely believe them.

If you do find you're struggling a little bit coming up with contradictory claims, you might want to recall similar stressful situations that produced the same kind of distressing automatic thoughts. In fact, in CBT this is not unusual. Many of my clients often keep thought diaries in which they record all kinds of unpleasant circumstances, which they then analyse along these lines. This way, they can be sure they've unearthed all the necessary, relevant and salient irrational thoughts (their hot thoughts) that reflect these situations. So, have a go at that.

It may also help to have a look at the following list of common thought distortions and see which ones apply. Usually, you'll feel some sort of resonance with the ones you physically or emotionally react to.

COMMON THINKING DISTORTIONS

The aim of CBT isn't to put a positive spin on a bleak, hopeless situation, but to evaluate stressful circumstances and logically analyse them by looking at all possible angles and potential explanations. This multi-factorial assessment gives you the power to formulate the appropriate course of action.

Since the principles of CBT are based on sound, scientific research, it's been possible to uncover the many different types of distorted thought processes that are activated in times of distress.

Version 1: Albert Ellis' Irrational Codes of Behaviour

We have talked about the two main pioneers of CBT: Albert Ellis and Aaron Beck. If you remember, I mentioned that each doctor formulated a slightly different account of the causes of emotional reasoning, although the basic tenets were much the same. The differences were more a matter of emphasis. You probably won't be surprised, therefore, to learn that they have slightly different views on the nature of distorted thoughts as well.

According to Albert Ellis, our thought distortions are born from irrational beliefs about rigid rules governing our behaviour. In his view, people hold ludicrously and unrealistically high expectations of themselves, other people and the world in general, becoming upset when things don't always turn out the way they expect. This leads to inner tension and distress, sometimes referred to as 'low frustration tolerance' or 'I-can't-stand-it-itis'.

His 1962 book, *Reason and Emotion in Psychotherapy* lists eleven of the more common irrational beliefs that people hold. They are:

1. It is a dire necessity for an adult to be loved or approved by virtually every other significant person in his or her community.

2. One should be thoroughly competent, adequate and achieving in all possible respects if one is to consider oneself worthwhile.

3. Certain people are bad, wicked, or villainous and should be severely blamed and punished for their villainy.

4. It is awful and catastrophic when things are not the way one would very much like them to be.

5. Human unhappiness is externally caused and people have little or no ability to control their sorrows and disturbances.

6. If something is or may be dangerous or fearsome one should be terribly concerned about it and should keep dwelling on the possibility of its occurring.

7. It is easier to avoid than to face certain life difficulties and self-responsibilities.

8. One should be dependent on others and need someone stronger than oneself on whom to rely.

9. One's past history is an all-important determiner of one's present behaviour, and because something once strongly affected one's life, it should definitely have a similar effect now.

10. One should become quite upset over other people's problems and disturbances.

11. There is invariably a right, precise and perfect solution to human problems and it is catastrophic if this perfect solution is not found.

None of us in fact lives in a perfect world, one that's free from cares, worries and woes, but for some reason many of us expect to. And because of our rigidly unrealistic rules and codes of behaviour, we imprison ourselves with the tyranny of 'shoulds' 'oughts' and 'musts':

1. I must do well and win the approval of other people. If I don't, I am substandard or inadequate.

2. Other people must treat me in precisely the manner I want or expect. If they don't, it's because they don't respect me or they look down on me.

3. My life must not be permeated by stresses, strains, or hassles. If it is, I won't be able to cope or tolerate.

In Ellis' view, the headaches and hassles we fret and frown over are actually nothing more than minor inconveniences. And yet they somehow get the better of us. Maybe it's because we're so busy squeezing more than is feasible out of a twenty-four-hour day, we often get caught up in petty concerns and magnify the stress they cause us.

How many of us are guilty of 'shoulding' and 'musting' and 'low frustration tolerancing' over really petty concerns?

There's no seat on the commuter train into work and you have to stand? Oh, no! The line in the bank is too long and you'll have to come back later in the day? I don't believe it! There's no record of your booking at the chi-chi restaurant? This can't be happening to me! Your car won't be ready for another week, because the part the mechanic ordered still hasn't arrived? I'm going to speak to the manager! The saleswoman at that exclusive designer boutique took one look at your outfit and sneered at you as if you were pond scum. How dare she treat me like that?

Of course, all these encounters and episodes are stressful and annoying. And inefficiency and rudeness make my blood boil at times too, but the point is this: keep things in perspective. No one died. Is there any real need to risk a coronary just because a jacket's not back from the cleaners? Well, is there?

Years ago, I heard a poignant anecdote on this subject, that was attributed to Ellis. Apparently, he was lecturing to a group of trainee R-E-B-T therapists and advocating his theories that human beings are capable of handling every situation if we only allow ourselves to think rationally, even about the worst cases of adversity and torture.

One of the students raised their hand and mentioned the holocaust. Surely, surely that was about as horrific an evil as there could possibly be? Ellis agreed. However, he pointed out that despite the villainy of the Nazis and the daily torture they inflicted in concentration camps, very few of the interred chose to end their lives. He found this interesting because many would under-standably have been going out of their minds from fear. Suicide would be the only viable means of escape. But they didn't opt for it. The majority, unbelievably, stuck it out. So, he told his students, if people were somehow able to persevere and carry on living in such a terrifying climate of hate and murderous intent, surely the rest of us can tolerate more mundane problems, no matter how much inconvenience they cause us?

Version Two: Aaron Beck's Selective Evidence

According to Aaron Beck, the origin of our disabling assumptions lies more with our tendency to select and look at only those bits of evidence that support our fears and anxieties. It might be tunnel-vision on our part, but every single time we're stressed, worked up, upset, frightened or experiencing any other state of heightened emotional arousal, everything else, every valid reason, logical interpretation or rational viewpoint, flies straight out of the window. It's only when we're calm that we can see and think clearly again.

Here are some of the more common kinds of thought distortions we're guilty of.

1. Black and white thinking

While the Beatles sang enthusiastically that all we need is love, the CBTer would argue that no man can live by bread alone – if you'll pardon this mixed metaphor. My point is that people get themselves in a muddle when they tend to view their circumstances in absolute terms, such as either good or bad. To these people, there's no middle ground. In psychology we call this tendency splitting.

The truth is, of course, situations or circumstances are rarely one extreme or the other. Usually there's some grey area. People are rarely 'completely useless' and circumstances aren't often 'totally hopeless'. If your automatic thoughts contain words like 'never', 'always', 'all', 'none' or 'ever', you're a black or white kind of thinker. Try instead to come up with counter examples to break this cognitive deadlock.

So, a deeply engrained irrational view such as 'I can't ever do anything right' turns into the more likely 'I might make mistakes from time to time, but last week I stayed up all night and finished that report. My boss read it through and thought it was excellent'.

2. Catastrophising

You've heard the expression 'making mountains out of molehills', I'm sure. Well, some people blow situations way out of proportion. They see disaster in even the most harmless of circumstances and exaggerate the significance of any event. Your boss barely acknowledged you one morning? Panic. It must mean he hates you and you're on the brink of getting the sack. More likely, he's distracted as he collects his thoughts for the upcoming meeting. Learning to maintain perspective is the key to counterbalance this kind of irrational thinking.

3. Personalising

Some people blame themselves for every situation that ends in disaster. 'It's all my fault' or 'I'm such an idiot' might as well be their mantra. Many victims of domestic violence have this kind of automatic thinking. They honestly believe that because they've cooked the 'wrong' dinner one night, failed to keep the home spotlessly clean or even dared to breathe, they're one hundred percent responsible for that fist that thumps them one.

People, however, don't have to live in dangerous situations to play the blame game. Personalising occurs in just about every situation. So, if you regularly carry the can for others or take full responsibility every time something falls apart, then step back and share the load.

4. Minimising

Another common disabling automatic thought is minimising. Many people with this built-in response filter out entirely their own positive traits, qualities, strengths and abilities, and home in instead on all their negative points. 'She'll never go out with a loser like me. What do I have to offer her?' 'I'll never get that job. People like me never get the good jobs.'

FINDING BALANCE:
CHANGING THOUGHT DISTORTIONS

With this new information on these common thought distortions, I now want you to reassess the automatic beliefs triggered by the stressful situation you identified. No doubt, you're already feeling less anxiety-ridden and better equipped to handle the tensions and distress caused by these circumstances.

If you're still not sure, don't worry. Don't be put off if Jack, Derek and all the others seemed to have grasped the CBT process quite easily. Remember, I've been working with them individually over several sessions and it took them a while to get the hang of it, too. With commitment and practice, you too will find it a breeze.

When people are just beginning to apply the CBT formula to their lives they often find the following list a useful tool for challenging any irrational beliefs.

1. What experiences do I have that demonstrate this thought is not one hundred percent true?
2. If a relative or a good friend held this particular view, what would I say to them?
3. Am I shouldering the blame for something which is not entirely my fault or a situation I don't have total control over?
4. Am I jumping to conclusions?
5. Am I focusing too much on my weaknesses?
6. Am I ignoring my strengths?
7. Am I trying to seek approval from someone I love or admire?
8. If this thought were true, what would be the worst-case scenario?
9. If a colleague, friend of family member knew I held this thought, what evidence would they come up with to contradict my beliefs?
10. Is this a case of low frustration tolerance?
11. In five years' time, would I be able to look at this situation differently?
12. When I have felt down, stressed or unhappy like this in the past, what helped me feel better?
13. Would I look at this situation differently if it didn't cause me stress? How?
14. Have I found myself in similar situations before? What did I learn from these experiences that could assist me now? How did I cope then?
15. Am I wishing situations could be different when I have no power to change them?

16. Do I have unrealistic expectations of myself or others?
17. What other possible explanations could there be for this situation?
18. Am I making mountains out of molehills?

What are your new constructive beliefs?

Now that you've had the opportunity to appraise your own thoughts in the light of these questions, I want you to write down your new, healthier, more balanced conclusions as my clients did in the examples above. Be sure to write them down.

What did you find? Do you feel different? Maybe your stresses involve other people. Yes, it's great to be liked and, yes, it's great to be held in high esteem by the people we admire and respect. However, try as we might, not everyone's going to think we're the bee's knees. And, yes, you might be kindness and decorum personified, always helpful, always considerate, but not everyone shares your sunny disposition. The fault doesn't necessarily lie with you. Maybe it's not personal. Maybe these people are difficult with everyone. Perhaps they lack social skills. Perhaps they feel it's inappropriate to be friendly and flattering.

When you find yourself in a situation in which you feel belittled or ignored, ask yourself: how valid is my conclusion? Is their hostile attitude just directed towards me or are they barking at everyone today? Do they behave like this to me all the time or are they just having a bad day? Have I actually done something to offend them? If so, what can I do to make amends?

Stepping back, taking a pause, you can more adequately assess whether your emotional conclusions are valid. In doing so, you will gain a breathing space to think about how you can respond next. You might want to remind yourself of all the people who do like and admire you to redress the balance. You could also keep the nasty, unpleasant encounter in perspective. So what if someone is rude or offhand with you? Is it really the end of the world? Are all your talents and traits to be automatically consigned to the dust heap because someone else demonstrated poor manners? Of course not. Keep these thoughts (and the NLP principles!) in mind, and even the most awkward encounters will be easy to deal with.

Sometimes it's not people who get us down. Sometimes life itself isn't smooth-running. There will be days when your car's broken down and there's no other way to take the kids to school. And, oh, yeah, you've got to take the dog to the vet and, yes, you promised you'd drop off a book for your mother at the library. All this before you have an important lunchtime business meeting.

Frustrating? Stressful? Irritating? We place so many demands on ourselves that we don't always recognise that we mere humans have limitations. So learn your limitations. Writing daily task lists, as we've mentioned before, is a perfect way to organise your day. As long as you manage to complete your priority duties, then other things can be put off until tomorrow or the next day.

Step Four: Reassessing your disabling emotions

Once you've come up with evidence contradictory to your automatic thoughts and re-examined your stressful situation in light of it, it's time to reassess your original emotional reactions.

Here's how my clients' emotions improved given their new insight:

	Before		**After**	
Jack	Jealous	7	Jealous	4
	Afraid	9	Afraid	4
	Powerless	8	Powerless	3
	Anger	6	Anger	2
	Useless	9	Useless	4

Derek	Fear	10	Fear	5
	Guilt	9	Guilt	5
	Self-loathing	9	Self-loathing	4
Melissa	Frustrated	8	Frustrated	5
	Pressurised	10	Pressurised	6
	Anxious	8	Anxious	5
Alison	Guilt	9	Guilt	3
	Stress	8	Stress	3
	Fear	8	Fear	2
	Loneliness	6	Loneliness	2
Edward	Anger	9	Anger	2
	Stressed	8	Stressed	3
	Powerless	8	Powerless	1
	Disappointed	7	Disappointed	1
Angela	Disappointment	9	Disappointment	5
	Rejected	9	Rejected	4
	Self-loathing	8	Self-loathing	3
	Lonely	8	Lonely	6
	Hopeless	9	Hopeless	3
Laura	Sadness	9	Sadness	7
	Jealousy	10	Jealousy	7
	Resentment	9	Resentment	5

You

As in my clients' cases, you probably noticed that your negative emotions didn't disappear entirely. Don't expect them to. Stressful situations are just that: Stressful. It's not possible to exorcise all your unpleasant feelings, nor is it necessary. The goal of CBT is to help people reframe disabling emotions, which entirely defeat, deflate or paralyse them, into more balanced feelings which individuals can work to overcome.

So, if someone makes a rude comment to you, it's okay to feel annoyed, irritated, maybe even shocked. But that's where it stops. No more allowing yourself to take the remarks so personally they cut you to the quick.

With CBT, thoughts like 'People never respect me', 'He must think so little of me to say something like that', or 'Others always hurt my feelings and put me down' are replaced with 'He's rude to everyone, not just me. It's his problem not mine', 'Am I really going to be that bothered if this person is rude to me? Is my whole self-esteem really based on rude comments by people I hardly know?', or 'So what if he doesn't like me? My partner, my friends and children all care about me. That's what counts'.

When it comes to shifting our disempowering beliefs, sometimes even just a little bit of additional information or a fresh perspective shifts our analysis of a situation by 180 degrees. Let's look at how my clients fared.

Jack: Viewing his situation through new eyes, Jack was able to grasp the point that, although finding a new job would be a difficult process, it wasn't an impossible one as he'd once believed. This insight gave him a renewed sense of confidence and we were able to look at different ways to facilitate the work search.

He was even able to admit that he had attended past interviews with such a glaring chip on his shoulder because of his firm convictions about ageism that he came across as obnoxious, surly and unpleasant. 'Not even I would have hired me!', Jack was able to joke.

It took a further two months for him to find a suitable job, but he got there in the end. Once his self-esteem had improved and his disabling biases were quelled, we were able first to look for positions he'd consider. Once he'd formulated this goal, we set out to achieve it. We examined his qualifications to see if they were suited to the desired posts and he decided to go on a short course to update himself with the industry's latest standards. He then brushed up on his interview techniques and we discussed the most likely questions and professional topics to be raised.

We next expanded his job search network. Originally Jack applied only for jobs he found advertised through the newspaper. Since most people find jobs through professional and social contacts, I encouraged him to join a job club for the unemployed executive, become a member of the local Chamber of Commerce and call his former work colleagues. Within the first week Jack had three interviews lined up and now he's once again gainfully and happily employed.

Derek: Surprisingly, given his recent history of severe anxiety and panic centred around the workplace, Derek made a quick recovery. After three sessions with me, he was back at work, in the same job that had caused him such distress as well. Not a bead of sweat. Not a panic attack in sight.

Once Derek was able to overcome his irrational beliefs about 'going crazy' and 'letting the wife down', we then had a chance to look at his work situation in a calmer, cooler light. Since his symptoms began with the workplace, it was the obvious starting point.

We soon discovered it wasn't working that was causing him anxiety, but his particular work. He'd spent his entire twenties and now part of his thirties working at a highly responsible, well-paid job and was simply fed up with being a drone. However, with a big mortgage and plans to start a family, Derek felt stuck in a permanent rut with the spectre of his youth fading fast. In the face of these combined pressures, panic was assured.

The way forward was fairly obvious. Derek needed either to rethink his career choice or reassess his priorities. Of course, switching his 'serious' job for something more carefree would only come at a cost. He'd probably have to consider selling his house and fancy car and live more modestly. Would his wife go along with that?

After careful consideration, Derek decided he wouldn't feel comfortable forcing her to give up her lifestyle, so instead we opted to look at ways to make his current job more palatable. I asked him to write down on a sheet of paper both the positive and negative features of his work position. Interestingly, the positives outweighed the negatives. He obviously enjoyed the high salary and prestige, but he also liked his colleagues, enjoyed his level of responsibility and the variety. The office was also a fairly short commuting distance away and the job came with all kinds of perks: a gym membership, good medical insurance and pension plan. The only real negative was the lack of excitement.

Since there was no point in throwing the proverbial baby out with the bath water, I asked Derek to explore possible outside interests that might instil a little buzz into what he saw as his humdrum existence. This way he could keep his job, but benefit from a more fulfilling life.

'You know, I've always wanted to learn how to fly,' he told me.

Within a week Derek had signed up for flying lessons. Two weeks later, he returned to work. No more panic.

Melissa: When Melissa changed her dysfunctional automatic thoughts, she realised that her fear of being unable to cope in Sydney was less daunting than she had at first imagined. Of course, accepting a promotion and moving to a foreign city are personal challenges to be carefully considered, but people face up to them every day and live to tell the tale. They don't just do them, they thrive on these new experiences.

To my mind, by even entertaining the thought of the new job, Melissa was outgrowing her previous sheltered existence. She was more than ready to taste some independence and see for herself what she was capable of, personally and professionally. This new job in Sydney was the perfect opportunity to spread her wings.

Once she was able to reassure herself that, in the worst-case scenario, she could come home any time and her close ties were just a phone call away, Melissa began to view the experience as a positive and exciting challenge. Even if Sydney were a huge disaster and she realised she was way out of her depth, she came around to the idea that she could still learn from this experience (there is no failure, only feedback). So, she accepted the job and was due to start six months down the road.

With so much time looming, I was concerned Melissa's resolve might start to crumble the closer her departure date approached, so we decided to take steps to prepare her for her new life in Oz. First, I asked her to contact everyone she knew who might have relatives, friends or colleagues living in Australia.

The next step on the agenda was to help Melissa develop a sense of independence before she left home. I wanted her to break free from her cosy, domestic comfort zone and meet new people. Undertake activities on her own. She joined a tennis club a fair distance away, spent one night a week by herself and even flew to New York alone for a long weekend of theatre and shopping.

After six months, not only did Melissa go to Sydney, not only did she love the experience, not only did she thrive in her new position – she decided to stay an extra two years.

Alison: Probably the biggest surprise for Alison in undertaking this exercise was realising the extent of her need for her mother's approval. Here she was, an adult herself, mother of two mature, bright, happy children – practically adults themselves. A successful career woman, acting like an adolescent desperate to hide a 'guilty' secret from her mother.

Our starting point was to discuss the appropriateness of Alison's anxieties about her relationship with her mother. Obviously, most of us care what our parents think of us, but Alison's fears were impacting on other areas of her life. She'd snap at her children because of the stress and considered withdrawing from a loving, caring relationship with a great woman.

Having explored the possible options Alison agreed she no longer wished to hide her sexuality and wanted to pursue her relationship with Paula. Since Alison's mother was fond of her gay cousin, she didn't seem to be averse to homosexuality *per se*, so that was encouraging. The problem with Alison's mother seemed to be her prudish attitudes towards sex in general; she seemed uncomfortable discussing anything to do with the subject. Is this so unusual? After all, how many adults have free and frank talks about their sex lives with their parents? Not a lot.

Maybe, therefore, Alison didn't have to sit her mother down and tell her about her lesbian orientation just yet. Perhaps her mother could gradually get to know Paula and see her playing a part in her daughter's life. She could either draw her own conclusions or, at a later stage, when Alison herself was comfortable in what would be her first lesbian relationship, daughter and mother could eventually have 'that chat'.

Edward: Edward was at least able to glean from this exercise that his hopes of happy families, although well-intentioned, were unrealistic and thoroughly misplaced. He'd been so wrapped up in his fantasy view of family life, feeling miserable that he couldn't obtain this vision, he'd totally overlooked two obvious facts.

First, happy families, in which no one ever raises a voice in anger or utters a harsh word, only exist on reruns of The Waltons. Second, his wife and mother could sort out their own battles. Unpleasant though it might be at times if these two didn't get along, couldn't stand the sight of one another, there was very little he could do or say to improve the situation.

Edward learned to stand his ground. Told them he was no longer getting involved. Let them know he wasn't prepared to take sides or hear another word on the subject. If they couldn't resolve their differences, he'd see them separately.

He really learned to assert himself!

Angela: Through this exercise, Angela was better able to see that her self-worth had been almost exclusively bound up with whether or not men, usually strangers in a bar or nightclub, noticed her. Since they ignored and rejected her, Angela assumed both that she was worthless and unattractive and therefore that she would end up alone.

Without wishing to make light of her unhappiness, I pointed out that if my self-esteem were based solely on the views of drunken, medallion-wearing barflies I'd never even seen before, then I'd probably be reaching for the whisky. Stuff the chocolate chip cookies!

As her therapist, I wanted to use the information gained from this exercise to help Angela develop confidence in her own right – irrespective of the man thing, expand her social life to meet men in more salubrious situations, and develop healthier eating patterns. Since her low self-esteem was the root of her late-night calorific comfort sessions, boosting Angela's confidence was an important step towards improving her physical well-being.

My first goal was to help her build her self-confidence. One of the first things I noticed was her striking theatrical personality. She was a natural thesp.

When I pointed out my observations to her, Angela agreed.

She told me that she'd been stage-struck since childhood and always wanted to perform, but somehow never quite got around to doing anything about it. Since she loved the idea of acting, she agreed to contact the local amateur dramatic society to find out about auditions.

As for the second matter on the agenda, we explored the pros and cons of meeting men in bars and nightclubs. We also talked about the NLP principle, if at first you don't succeed, try something different, and since these venues had proved dismal failures, I asked Angela to think of the ways her friends and family members had met their partners. She rattled off the gym, local politics, the sailing club and the Chamber of Commerce. Not a bar or night club among them. In other words, her family and friends had met their spouses through a common, mutually enjoyable activity. It makes sense – when people share the same interests, they tend to have a natural rapport and conversation flows easily. With this in mind, Angela said she's always been interested in learning the tango and had just seen some classes advertised in the local newspaper. I encouraged her to sign up and recommended that for the next six months, she put a dating ban on herself. This would take the pressure off her and help her get to know men as individuals first.

Finally, we tackled her unhealthy eating patterns. I recommended a dietician who'd give her all the essential nutritional information she'd need and a healthy eating plan for her to follow. We also discussed distraction activities, such as calling a friend and house-cleaning, to defuse stress when she felt like binge-eating.

I last spoke to Angela about four months ago. She reported feeling happy, healthy and doing fine. She had the lead in the local play and was tangoing to her heart's content. She also had a full circle of friends, both male and female, and was more than content to remain single for a little while yet.

Laura: Who could not feel sympathy for Laura and her painful dilemma about motherhood? It is such a powerful, emotionally laden concept and very much bound up with definitions of womanhood. From early childhood most young girls grow up with notions of motherhood as central to their life script and it is a biological injustice that females' reproductive years are so limited in comparison with men's.

This exercise helped Laura come to terms with her finite fertility and also to explore some of the other child-rearing options available to her. We talked about egg donation, freezing eggs, adoption and fostering, and Laura realised that although her preference would be a child genetically her own, these possibilities were also viable alternatives for her. As a result, she came to see that her biological clock wasn't quite the time bomb she had once been panicking about.

We also talked a little bit about her worries and concerns about being 'defective' or 'second-rate' female goods if she never became a mother. From the example she gave of a childless professional aunt who led a rich, fulfilling life, Laura was able to provide herself with an important role model. Being childless might well be painful, but life holds a variety of riches and she could develop as a woman in other ways.

With this new-found sense of balance and inner peace, I decided to press Laura about a concern I had: her relationship with Richard. Although they were clearly very devoted to one another, I found it odd that she was left to deal with these painful worries and fears about childlessness all by herself. Surely he couldn't be so insensitive as to brush aside and dismiss something so important to Laura as her desire for motherhood? Did she feel she had an equal say in this relationship or was Richard the one in charge? How would she feel in ten years' time should Richard all of a sudden desire fatherhood? What if he left her some day to satisfy a need to have children? Would she feel cheated and resentful then?

After considering these questions, Laura came to realise just how much power Richard wielded. He made all the major decisions and she went along with them. The houses they bought. Their holiday destinations. Marriage and children – or not as the case was. Curiously, Laura never had a say or a vote in any of it. I'm not suggesting that Richard was a bad person, but this relationship was seriously unbalanced and Laura was left feeling isolated and insignificant.

I suggested that confidence and assertiveness were goals she might want to consider for her relationship. Since the strongest unions between men and women are based on mutual goals and ambitions, I also asked Laura to write down all the characteristics and qualities she wanted in her ideal partner. I suggested she might want to talk to Richard and explain what her goals were for their relationship to see what they could work out. If he couldn't oblige, then Laura would have to decide if she was content to stay with a man who was dictating her life or should she begin thinking about finding a new partner whose vision of a relationship was the same as hers.

Laura didn't exactly go home and throw down the gauntlet at Richard's feet or issue ultimatums, but she started asserting her needs and desires more and more. Within a few months of doing so, she began to feel that she and Richard were finally equal partners. So much so, that she sat him down to discuss and plan their future. Starting with their engagement.

You: Now it's your turn. Take a few minutes to think about the ways in which this CBT exercise has changed your perceptions of the stressful situation you identified. How will you react differently in future to similar circumstances as a result? How have your beliefs about yourself been transformed? What other personal benefits have you gained through changing your beliefs?

Step Five: Maximising the benefits of your new beliefs

When we hold healthy, enabling beliefs about ourselves and the world around us, we can pretty much achieve anything we set our minds to. Once we've learned how to tackle our fears, no challenge is insurmountable. No goal too intimidating. No ambition too lofty.

In learning how to achieve this CBT exercise, my clients invariably feel they've been given a new lease on life. Many, indeed, claim that merely acquiring the skill of identifying and challenging automatic destructive thoughts and replacing them with healthier, enabling balanced beliefs is sufficient for them to gain all the confidence they require to handle stressful situations and achieve their personal aims and ambitions.

The key to continued CBT success, however, is practice. Like any new skill, you have to keep fine-tuning and regularly honing it, otherwise the benefits start to fade away. With CBT, it's no different. So, I suggest you do this exercise at least three times a week to ensure you've got the hang of it. The more you do it, the easier it will become and the more you'll reap the rewards. Some of my clients find it useful to keep a diary just for this purpose. I recommend you block off a series of columns and pre-label them: situation, physical feelings, behaviours, emotions, automatic thoughts, supporting evidence, challenging evidence, more balanced cognitions, and revised emotional assessment. This way, the process will be easily laid out for you.

Thought-challenging recap

1. Always make sure the situation you've described is as specific as possible.
2. When you identify the corresponding physical feelings, behaviours and emotions, ensure that they accurately reflect your reactions.

3. It's important to rate your moods as well.
4. Identify as many automatic thoughts as you can and circle the 'hot thought' or most powerful belief if there is one.
5. Write down evidence in support of each perception.
6. Use facts not interpretations.
7. In challenging these beliefs, evaluate the evidence from as many perspectives as possible.
8. Avoid using positive thinking when thought challenging, and only use contradicting evidence that is convincing to you.
9. Make sure your new, balanced explanation is believable.
10. Re-rate your moods following your new beliefs.

GREATEST SOURCES OF JOY

Falling in love	Passing an exam
Recovering from illness	Going on holiday
Getting engaged/married	Birth of a child
Winning some money	Job promotion
Socialising with friends	Getting a new job
Making up with a partner following an argument	

WEEK NINE:
The Final Touches

Welcome to the final furlong. How are you feeling? The theme of the previous two weeks, identifying and challenging automatic beliefs, is pretty powerful stuff. Even at this stage, when tackling and transforming your negative, self-defeating cognitions is still fairly new to you, I'm sure you can appreciate the power of this amazing process. Take a few moments now to think about some other stressful occasions that have plagued you in the past. In what ways do you see them differently now? How do you see yourself differently? How are you able to overcome past or future adversity as a result of these new skills?

For the final week, I'd like you to carry on with the following tasks and goals.

1. Looking after your health
2. Thirty minutes of physical exercise at least three times per week
3. Ten to fifteen minutes relaxation every day
4. Improving sleep
5. Mirror exercise
6. Random acts of smiling
7. Exchanging good news

8. Thirty minutes a week on your hobby
9. Blue dot exercise
10. Keep up with daily task list
11. Time for reflection
12. Thought challenging exercises at least three times per week

This week's focus is on winding down the program and the exercises here are designed to give you another opportunity for reflection. About the direction of your life. About your goals. About your dreams.

EXERCISE 31:
LIFE BALANCE

We start with the life balance exercise. By participating in this programme, you've already taken the first important steps towards realising your hopes and goals. And, by now, because of the topics we've covered and the new skills you've developed, you're probably in the best physical and mental shape you've ever been in to go out and really make your mark in this world.

So, on a piece of blank paper, I want you to draw a straight line down the middle. On the left-hand side, write 'List One' at the top and take a few moments to think about all the activities, interests, hobbies and pastimes, both past and present, that really make you happy. The ones that fill your life with joy and excitement. So much so, you'd love to devote all your time to them if you could. What would they be? Painting and drawing? Gardening? Amateur dramatics? Socialising with friends? Cooking? Travelling? Once you've decided, write them all down under 'List One'.

Next, I want you to think about all the reasons why these activities give you such pleasure. What makes them so worthwhile?

Are they challenging? Do they make you feel competent, special or inspired? Do they give you a sense of accomplishment? Do you meet like-minded people? Whatever your reasons, write them all down underneath the activities.

In the next step, I want you to think about all the people, both past and present, who are special to you. Maybe you're thinking of your childhood best friend of favourite teacher. Perhaps you feel particularly close to your partner or another relative. Maybe you identify with someone who has similar interests or experiences. Then, write all their names down in 'List One'.

With these people in mind, I now want you to reflect on all the reasons why their presence in your life is (or has been) so positive. In what ways do they make you feel good about yourself? Do they accept you for who you are? Have they stood by you when others haven't? Have they inspired you to achieve your goals? Do you have shared interests in common? Do they make you feel appreciated and special?

Once you've decided, write down all the reasons underneath their names.

Now, turn to 'List Two', which should be subtitled 'Life's too short'. This part of the exercise is similar, but there's a twist. This time, we're going to concentrate on the activities and people who exert a *negative* influence on our lives. The first step is to identify all those duties and responsibilities that are a real chore. This could be any activity as long as the very thought of it fills you with dread, irritation or boredom. What fits this bill? Your job? Certain aspects of your work? Domestic duties? Commuting to your office? Once you've made up your mind, write them all down under 'List Two'.

Then I want you to think about all the reasons why you deplore these activities. What's so unappealing about them? Do they leave you feeling undervalued? Do you feel exploited? Are they just plain tedious and dull? Whatever thoughts and feelings are generated, write them all down.

Now, turn to the people, either past or present, whose very influence is somehow toxic to you. Who brings out the worst in you? Who has made you feel bad about yourself and your abilities in the past? Bosses? Teachers? Former lovers? A friend who's betrayed you? Work colleagues? Relatives? Write them all down.

Once again, with these names in mind, I want you to think about all the reasons why they're so unpleasant to you. Do you feel undermined? Drained by their constant demands? Unappreciated? Insecure? Pushed around? Unable to stand up for yourself? Inadequate? Stressed? Rejected? Undermined? Guilty? Write down all your thoughts and feelings that spring to mind.

Once you've completed both lists, I want you to compare and contrast the positive and negative forces in your life. Are the lists balanced? Or are your personal resources being overwhelmingly depleted and drained by disagreeable chores and people? If so, what ways can you come up with to help redress this balance? How can your life be made more palatable and pleasurable? What would you like to do?

Unfortunately, wishing for a magic wand to banish these malignant forces from our lives once and for all is not an option. We have to come up with our own proactive strategies to handle these negative life forces. So, think about the following solutions. We might not be able to avoid the chores or the grumps, but we have more control over the situations than we think.

First, you need to eliminate, reduce or share these burdens with others. So, take a good, hard look at the amount of time you spend on unpleasant chores and people and think about why they're invading your space. Are you compensating for the slackers in your life? Are you worried they won't get seen to otherwise? Have you convinced yourself that no one else could do as good a job as you? If so, then perhaps you need to learn to let go and delegate responsibility to others.

Maybe instead you need to assert yourself. Learn to say no

when others encroach on your time, making demands. Standing up for yourself can be daunting, but it's not as intimidating as it sounds. I often advise my clients to use this good cop-out clause for pushy people. Instead of saying no, say, 'I'll have to get back to you'. If they persist or become more badgering, which they probably will, you'll be fine as long as you stick to that line. Even parrot fashion. They'll get the message soon enough.

Why not also try increasing the amount of time you spend on the activities and the people you really enjoy? Simple, obvious and very effective.

If something or someone disagreeable is absolutely un-avoidable and you have no choice but to grit your teeth, smile and get through it, then plan something really enjoyable afterwards. A reward.

EXERCISE 32:
YOUR LIFE IN REVIEW

Now that you've had a chance to clarify your life's obligations and redress the balance of your positive and negative commitments, I want you to take a broader perspective. Explore the bigger picture. Find out where your life's going. In psychology, we call this the life review exercise. It's enormously helpful for shaping our future course, motivating us and giving us direction. Take some blank sheets of paper and think about your answers to the following questions.

1. What are all your secret dreams and hopes, both large and small?
2. What are your special abilities, gifts and strengths?
3. What traits and characteristics would you like to develop in yourself?
4. How would you describe the perfect lifestyle?

5. What would you like to experience in your lifetime?
6. What are your emotional, intellectual, physical and spiritual needs?
7. In what ways are you growing as a person?
8. Do you find your life challenging enough?
9. Is your life rewarding enough?
10. Is your life loving enough?
11. If you found out you only had a year to live, what changes would you make?

The life review exercise helps people identify and tap into any unfulfilled aims and ambitions they might have. Sometimes, it's not a question of articulating goals but figuring out the steps to achieve them that's the real problem. But not to worry. Keeping yourself motivated, focused and organised really are the key steps to achieving success. Getting started is often a hurdle also, but this obstacle is so easy to overcome. The secret is to model yourself after people who've achieved success in your chosen field. They've already illustrated the most effective methods.

In the meantime, it's important you think about success and what it means to you. Answering the following questions should help clarify your mind:

1. How do you define success?
2. What are the most important lessons you've learned about success in your own life?
3. What are the limitations of success?
4. How will success change your life?
5. How will you know when you've achieved success? Status? Money? Independence?
6. Who is the most successful person you know or know of?
7. What is so attractive to you about this person's success?
8. How important is success for your personal happiness?

Exercise 33:
The fifth NLP principle

As you contemplate how you want to live your life from now and how not to, I want you to turn your thoughts to the final NLP principle: **If at first you don't succeed, try something different**.

Think back to my clients. Jack had no luck finding work through newspaper advertisements. He joined a job club, called old friends in his industry and became a member of the Chamber of Commerce. He also signed up for a training course to brush up his skills and I coached him on interview techniques. Hard work? Sure. Lots of effort? You bet. In the end, the blood, sweat and tears paid off. Jack was no longer an unemployment statistic.

Now it's your turn. I want you to think about some obstacle in your life and write down the strategy you've employed to overcome it. Maybe you're trying to find yourself a better job but only restrict your search to newspaper advertisements, or perhaps you're doing your damnedest to lose weight but the diet that melts the fat away from your mother and best friend has made no difference at all to your waistline and hips.

If your attempts to achieve your goal have been thwarted or have left you feeling discouraged, don't give up. Try something different. Write down at least three other ways that could help you solve your problem.

Exercise 34:
The happiness questionnaire – again

Well, that's it. Congratulations on completing this course. Before we come to a close, why don't you see how far you've progressed in terms of your emotional well-being over the past couple of months?

How happy are you now? Take the Happiness Questionnaire one more time and find out. Don't consult your earlier answers until you finish.

1. I am busier than other people. ☐

2. I have numerous leisure activities to occupy me. ☐

3. I am nearly always 'on the go'. ☐

4. I definitely have more friends than most people. ☐

5. I socialise several times in the average week. ☐

6. I really love spending time with other people. ☐

7. I find my work extremely interesting. ☐

8. Time usually flies when I'm working. ☐

9. I usually work very efficiently. ☐

10. My life is carefully organised. ☐

11. I can nearly always lay my hands on important documents. ☐

12. I usually have enough time each week to do what I want to do. ☐

13. I worry more than most people. ☐

14. I usually find it impossible to keep worrying thoughts out of my mind. ☐

15. Life is a very worrying business. ☐

16. I take life very much as it comes. ☐

17. I do not have any great unfulfilled aspirations. ☐

18. I expect the future to be very much like the past. ☐

19. I am generally very optimistic about things. ☐

20. I am confident that my life will turn out well. ☐

21. I generally anticipate that things will turn out for the best. ☐

22. I think about the present much more than I do about the past or the future. ☐

23. The 'here and now' is of absorbing interest. ☐

24. I always try to live 'for the moment'. ☐

25. My friends regard me as well-adjusted. ☐

26. I am nearly always cheerful. ☐

27. I generally 'bounce back' from adversity. ☐

28. I am more outgoing than most people. ☐

29. People think of me as being very sociable. ☐

30. I am a particularly friendly person. ☐

31. I never 'put on an act' with other people. ☐

32. I am content just to be myself. ☐

33. I have no wish to be like anyone else. ☐

34. I do not feel like my problems are insuperable. ☐

35. I do not waste any of my time envying other people. ☐

36. I very rarely experience frustration and anger. ☐

37. I have an intimate relationship. ☐

38. My family life has been very loving. ☐

39. I have more exceptionally close friends than most other people.

40. I always do what I can to be happy.

41. I regard being happy as the main goal in life.

42. I would rather live in ignorant bliss than be a miserable genius.

43. I am much happier than most people.

44. I am somewhat unhappy much of the time.

45. I wish I could be happier.

The scoring system is obviously the same as before. How did both sets of overall scores compare? What about those for the specific sections? In what areas did your levels of happiness really improve?

It's important to keep in mind that everybody's progress is different, so there are no right or wrong answers. While some people find a dramatic improvement in their emotional well-being, others see a more modest change. Some find improvement in all aspects of their life, while others experience change only in certain areas. Remember, we're not aiming for a quick fix, this course was designed to improve your overall sense of well-being, it's the long-term benefits we're after.

Now that you've had a chance to compare your scores, take a few moments to think about the impact this program has had on your life. Here's what some of my previous clients have had to say on the matter. In what ways do their experiences match your own? In what ways were your expectations met?

I'm surprised at how much I really enjoyed this course. At first I wasn't so sure. I thought the exercises would be pointless and the information useless. But I was wrong. I've learned to think more about my emotions and understand now that I have more control over them, my thoughts and my life.

I used to think I had to accept my lot in life. That happiness, dreams and a better life were for other people, not me. I'm glad I was proved wrong. Life holds so much more excitement and promise for me now. My only regret is I didn't know about this program before.

I always knew I wanted more. I always wanted to make real changes in my life, but never knew how to start. I've also spent so much of my time looking after other people and now realise that my needs are important too.

I rediscovered my love of music. I'd forgotten how much I enjoyed playing the flute and going to concerts. It's been a while, but I've started taking lessons again and have joined a local orchestra.

I'm in better shape physically and look after my health much more. I feel better, I look better and have gained so much confidence even in the past few weeks.

I used to expect other people to take charge of my life. It was so frustrating and made me irritable and stressed. I'm so much more relaxed, much nicer to be around.

I learned a lot about myself and my reactions to other people. I'm quite sensitive and tend to get upset a lot of the time. This course helped teach me to cope in these situations. Instead of feeling helpless, I'm in the driver's seat. I'm more confident and more relaxed. Even my boss has commented.

I just smile so much more. I get up and look forward to the day. I used to grumble a lot about the state of the world and all that negativity was doing my head in. Life's still full of problems, but I see the positive side of things much more.

I learned that all those things I was told as a child, by teachers and my father, about how I could never amount to anything, just no longer applied. I'd been insecure for so long and never gave myself any credit for my abilities. Now I focus on my strengths and dare to take challenges.

I've learned I can *choose* to be happy. Misery is only an option.

You've only just begun . . .

You've come so far. So, don't stop now. To continue on the path of empowerment and personal satisfaction, I strongly recommend that you carry on with certain aspects of the program:

1. Looking after your health
2. Thirty minutes of physical exercise at least three times per week
3. Ten to fifteen minutes' relaxation every day
4. Improving sleep
5. Mirror exercise
6. Random acts of smiling
7. Exchanging good news
8. Thirty minutes a week on your hobby

9. Blue dot exercise
10. Keep up with daily task list
11. Time for reflection
12. Recording and challenging automatic thoughts at least three times per week

The more you incorporate these tasks into your daily life, the more your happiness will continue to blossom. But you didn't need me to tell you that, did you? Keep on, keeping on being happy.